The Year of the
GOAT

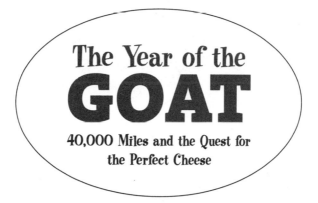

The Year of the
GOAT

40,000 Miles and the Quest for
the Perfect Cheese

Margaret Hathaway

Photographs by Karl Schatz

THE LYONS PRESS
Guilford, Connecticut
An imprint of the Globe Pequot Press

The Lyons Press is an imprint of The Globe Pequot Press.

10 9 8 7 6 5 4 3 2

Printed in the United States of America

ISBN 978-1-59921-021-6

Library of Congress Cataloging-in-Publication Data is available on file.

For Charlotte

Contents

Introduction

When I lived in New York, I thought of farming as the return to a simpler life. I imagined the people who sold cheese, greens, and homemade sausage at the market in Union Square to have lives much different from my own: engaged in the rhythm of the seasons, elevated through their literal roots to a higher spiritual plane. I knew there were hardships—the plight of the American small farmer was enough of a catchphrase to make that obvious—but other than weather and disease, I had no idea what they were. I saw them with their battered trucks and dirt-streaked work pants, and I imagined that their lives had a kind of purity of intention that mine lacked. I thought their days must be governed by the needs of their animals and plants, that once a week they would make the trip into the city, but otherwise they would simply work the land. In my mind, this existence was somehow less complex and cluttered than my own.

In the early months of 2003, my boyfriend, Karl, and I began to yearn for this kind of life. The feeling had built gradually within each of us, unspoken, and by the time we discussed it, we were both in its thrall: we wanted a quieter life.

We lived at the time in Brooklyn and worked in Manhattan at jobs we enjoyed. Karl was the picture editor for Time.com, the Web site for *Time* magazine. I was a manager at the Magnolia Bakery, a West Village landmark that had earned its reputation by making homey sweets that reminded patrons of their childhood, lived or imagined.

We were very much engaged in the city, beginning our days at the Fort Greene dog park, scanning the *Voice* and *Time Out New York* for things to do in the evenings, ordering takeout from the cornucopian drawer of menus in our kitchen. (Only in New York do your delivery choices include sushi, Dixie, and Senegalese.) We had a life that in many ways was fulfilling: a dog, the bottom story of an old brownstone, a large circle of friends, enough money to eat well and take interesting vacations. But at the same time our priorities were shifting, and as our domestic life assumed a new weight, we began to question some of our choices.

When we moved in together in the fall of 2002, our lives had begun to center less on the delights of the city and more on the comforts of home. We had adopted a puppy, and his needs precluded long nights out. Instead, we painted our apartment and invited friends over for lavish dinners, cracking the spine of Julia Child's *Mastering the Art of French Cooking* to offer our unsuspecting guests stuffed shoulder of lamb, *daube de boeuf*, and duck braised with chestnuts and cabbage. Our meals, whether with friends or alone, stretched for hours over several courses. We still went to exhibits and concerts, but the urgency to take part in every opportunity the city could offer had been supplanted by a satisfaction in nesting.

As the winter stretched on, and that first hushing magic of snowfall was replaced by a harsh, biting cold, this became especially true. The gray-capped snow and leaden skies felt dirty and oppressive; unshakable chills and deep pools of exhausted slush made the days bleak and dingy. Late blizzards shut down public transportation and sent Karl out on cross-country skis to walk the dog. At the bakery, we had to cover the checkerboard floor with flattened cardboard to soak up the slop tracked in by every damp boot. The subway was slick with iced grime, and it seemed as though each fellow rider was angry. When we weren't at work, Karl and I just wanted to be at home.

In late January I spent several days in upstate New York at the restored farmhouse of my friend and Magnolia's owner, Allysa Torey. We were working on a cookbook she was writing and spent most of the time indoors at the dining room table, which was covered in recipes and Post-it notes. But the mere fact of being in the country caused a dramatic change in my mood. Though I was sitting with my boss, working for eight hours at a stretch, the glimpse through the window over her shoulder of dried cornstalks in a field made me breathe a little deeper. The winter claustrophobia that had settled within me was alleviated, not by spring, but by space.

I came back to the city with a dream of the country. I felt like a different person when I was out of New York: my neck relaxed, my head cleared. In contrast to the frantic pace of my city life with its lists and anxieties and headaches, this brief escape brought me calm and a keen focus. Days in the country seemed longer and more expansive, suffused somehow with a sense of possibility.

Coming back, I wondered what sort of people Karl and I would be if we lived in the country. I imagined us in a town like Allysa's, living in a many-roomed old house with a wide porch and a big garden. Our dog Godfrey would have room to romp in the fields; I would watch him from a distance while I hung out laundry or darned socks or made pickles. Though I'd only known Karl as a city person, when we'd first met he'd kept a small garden behind his apartment, and I'd seen his delight tending tomatoes, hollyhocks, and strawberries. I could easily imagine him puttering around the yard or tinkering with a lawnmower, wearing a wide-brimmed straw hat and wiping sweat from his brow with a bandanna. The fantasy included babies and Sunday dinners and like-minded neighbors who would drop by for late-morning coffee.

My daydreams were an amalgam of memories from my grandmother's house and *Charlotte's Web*—an existence bustling with people and chores but tidy and orderly, curtains ironed, bathrooms scrubbed. It was very 1950s, embarrassingly coated in gender stereotypes, but it was a captivating dream. I was sure that life would feel easier in the country, even if our daily tasks were just as hard. Returning to the present, to our urban livelihoods and rhythms, I wondered what we could do to support ourselves in a rural community.

I shared the vision with Karl, who is an animal lover, and it was he who hit upon the idea of farming, though at first it was kind of a joke. It was something fun to think about, and it was a fantasy that fueled us through the winter. When the weather was ugly or someone on the street was rude, we could seek solace in our farm.

About this time, the bakery received a case of samples from Ronnybrook Farm, a small New York dairy. The story of Ronnybrook was one that, in the following year, would become very familiar to me: a small family farm, squeezed on all sides by corporate dairies and agribusiness, had found a niche. At Ronnybrook Farm, their tactic had been to beautify their packaging, diversify their products, and, most important, to keep their milk as natural as possible. What the dairy's salesperson dropped off at Magnolia was a plastic crate filled with glass bottles of milk, yogurts, fresh cheeses, and a paper-wrapped block of sweet butter. It was amazing. The flavor of the milk reminded you of its origins; it wasn't exactly that it tasted of grass and sky, but something in it recalled its source. There was a richness and a complexity about it that I had ceased to expect from milk. In the end, we couldn't switch to Ronnybrook's milk at the bakery, but their example had changed something within me. It suddenly seemed possible to live out the dreams we had been concocting, to live both off the land and closer to it. If other people were making a go of it as farmers, I thought, why couldn't we?

At home, Karl and I began to talk seriously about farming and about the possible niches we could find and fill. Cows were out of the question for a number of reasons: they are too large, there are too many farms like Ronnybrook already in existence, and we didn't feel drawn to them by any kind of cosmic tug. Then we began to talk about goats.

We both love goat cheese, and the more we talked, the more we found the idea of goats oddly compelling. Karl had visited a goat dairy in the Berkshires, and from that experience he easily imagined himself caring for a small herd. I wanted to make something, and envisioned myself in the earthiest of situations, milking animals and then turning that milk into something pungent and fabulous. As a very small child I had been to a cheese cave in France where wooden hoops formed cheeses that aged against dank stone. In retrospect it's embarrassing, but when I thought of making cheese, that was my point of reference, and it seemed wonderful.

I felt, too, as though I had been moving in this direction—toward a cave in the country—since nearly the beginning of my life in New York. When I had first moved to the city, I worked for a year as an assistant to a cookbook editor. I realized during that time that while I was reading manuscripts about food, what I really wanted to be doing was preparing it. There was a sterility to my life in an office that made me feel profoundly disconnected from the world around me. My first remedy was to quit that job, to trade in silk scarves for vintage cotton kerchiefs, and start working at Magnolia where my days were filled with frosting, conversation, and natural light. There were parts of me that still loved this life, but an increasingly larger part of me wanted a stronger connection to my environment than I could ever have in the city. As Karl and I talked about goats, we both became seduced by the image of ourselves as farmers and cheese makers, escaping from our current lives and creating, in the country, better versions of ourselves.

We began to do some empirical research. On reconnaissance missions to the cheese counters at Zabar's and Fairway market, we sampled different types of goat cheese. There were fresh chèvres, the mild, crumbling, luminous white cheese most people associate with goats. We found them blended with honey, rolled in vegetable ash, and swirled through with herbs, some forming a beautiful loose spiral of deep green and white. One called Madame Chèvre, from Woolwich Dairy in Canada, came already packaged with various accompaniments, like roasted red peppers and spiced cranberries. There were aged and softly running crottins, small, flat disks of pungent cheese whose name derives from the French word for animal droppings. There was even a nutty brown cheese from Norway that had the dense consistency and concentrated sweetness of caramel. At Gourmet Garage, I found several flavors of goat's milk yogurt from Redwood Hill Farm in California. At our local Pathmark grocery store, I even found ultrapasteurized fluid goat milk from Meyenberg, another California dairy.

We experimented, substituting goat's milk in things like hot chocolate and rice pudding. While the processing of the milk had gotten rid of any trace of a goaty flavor, there were definitely some additions that went well and others that did not. We found that we liked goat's milk with chocolate, cinnamon, honey, mint, rosemary, and, weirdly, grapes. We didn't much care for it with citrus, and found that quiche made with goat's milk was a little strange (though, to be fair to the goat's milk, I also put in Gruyère, and it may have been the combination of flavors that clashed).

We also started to do some Internet research about dairy goats and small farming. What we turned up was in many ways discouraging: land was outrageously expensive, the variety of dairy goats was overwhelming, and making interesting cheeses looked much harder on the computer screen than it had in my childhood memory. The projected startup cost of a U.S. Department of Agriculture (USDA)-inspected Grade A dairy, which is the only kind that can legally ship products across state lines, was about a quarter of a million dollars. That was just for the equipment and animals; a farm on which to put them would at least double the cost. Looking at online real estate ads, we found trim dairies, rambling farmsteads, empty parcels of land, all bearing price tags with more zeros than we could contemplate.

"Good God," I would breathe, leaning over Karl's desk chair to look at listings that were progressively farther from our means. Any way you look at it, $500,000 is a startling amount of money, but it is especially so when you're looking at it from a rented one-bedroom apartment in Brooklyn. Without money to pursue it, we felt the dairy dream slipping from our grasp.

By this point, however, we had become goat people. Everywhere we looked, they seemed to rear their horned heads. In an afternoon at the Met, what I saw was not an accumulation of fine art, but rather goats capering across the swollen jugs of red and black amphorae, gauzy Impressionist goats chewing their cud, glazed Chinese goats corralled in an ancient earthenware pen. Cutting through the food court at Grand Central, my eyes rested on the curried goat sign at Golden Krust. The U.S. Postal Service had just issued goat stamps for the Chinese New Year; a Gambian baker at Magnolia brought leftover goat stew for lunch. Goats were everywhere.

We could not give up the dream of ourselves as goat farmers. We were possessed by the idea, and our hopes had gone so far into the country that our daily city lives seemed schizophrenic and disappointing. Celebrity spottings at the bakery, the startup of *Time*'s softball season, chicken and fried yucca from our favorite Peruvian restaurant—things that had once been cheerful distractions no longer brought that little zip to our lives. We moped around the apartment, feeling cramped in rooms that had once seemed spacious. We snapped at each other, as though blaming one another for inadequacies that (we imagined) had precluded acting on the fantasy. But we simply couldn't find an angle that would put this goat dream into a manageable order. Karl had the idea of apprenticing ourselves but didn't know where to begin. I thought of trying to coerce family members into becoming business partners, but no one was really interested. We both tossed out the idea of simply moving to a small town and seeing what happened.

In May we took a vacation to South Africa, trying to shake off our goat malaise with an adventure. Ironically, South Africa is the heart of the international meat goat industry, and in retrospect, the vacation was a little like trying to escape cattle by going to rural Kansas. At the time, however, it was just the nudge we needed to push us out of inertia. For two weeks, we went on photo safaris, toured vineyards, and swam with penguins. We returned to New York refreshed, Karl excited by the photos he'd taken and I by the serendipity of travel. After months of funk, we felt fun again.

Dr. Fraum, Karl's therapist, had been listening to the goat saga— its wild speculations, curious revelations, crashing defeats—twice weekly for many months. He had been patient throughout the spring, making the appropriate noises of encouragement and skepticism, but in late May, upon our joyful return from Africa, he made a bold suggestion: what if we were to take a year to explore the goat world? We could have adventures, take photographs, record our thoughts, and at the end, if we made it, we could decide whether devoting our lives to agriculture was really the answer. It wouldn't bring us any closer to the down payment on a farm, but after a year we might realize that a farm wasn't what we wanted.

In retrospect, it seems likely that Dr. Fraum was not making a serious suggestion but rather throwing out the idea casually to assess our levels of both commitment and desperation. But whatever his intention, for us it was a revelation. Karl and I found in his idea the germ of a plan—here was a way to our dream! Dr. Fraum tossed a Rorschach blot in front of us, and in it we saw goats and a path out of the city.

Through a fortuitous series of events—most notably the loan of a car and a house by our parents—by summer we were in a position to leave New York and travel the country. In August of 2003, six months into the zodiacal Year of the Goat, we began our own.

Chapter 1

W̲e start our journey before leaving New York with a visit to Max McCalman at the restaurant Picholine. Max is the author of *The Cheese Plate*, and as the maître fromager at both Picholine and its sister restaurant, Artisanal Fromagerie and Bistro, he is a recognized authority on cheese. We meet with him in the late afternoon of a muggy August day as he arranges the evening's cheese cart in a climate-controlled room that functions as the restaurant's wine cellar. Periodically through our conversation, Max disappears into his adjacent cheese cave, emerging with a pungent paper-wrapped lump that he sniffs, pokes, and carves before arranging it on the marble slab of his cart. We have chosen Max for precisely this kind of single-minded distraction. His devotion to cheese, and specifically to maintaining its integrity through proper storage and handling, is legendary among foodies. What we hope to learn from him is some background on American goat cheese. We want to know the issues facing American cheese makers, the varieties of cheese they are producing, and the operations he thinks we should visit.

Max is a slight man, and in appearance and bearing he seems European. He arranges his cart in shirtsleeves and a tie, and somehow the casual dignity of his attire is in no way undermined by the fact that what he is doing, at base, is evaluating the progress of bacteria.

The process of cheese making is achieved in roughly four steps: acidification of the milk; coagulation, or curdling; cutting and draining; and ripening, or maturing, the cheese. All cheese is acidified and curdled. In the first step, the milk is warmed and a bacteria that produces lactic acid is introduced. The bacteria can be one of many kinds, and the ultimate flavor of the cheese is dependent upon which culture is used. When the milk has acidified, or ripened, another agent—either rennet or a vegetable extract—is added to coagulate the milk. In this second step, the milk curdles, and the whey separates from the curds. The whey is generally discarded (or cooked to make ricotta), and the curds are cut and drained.

It is at this stage that the most significant variations between cheeses occur. Depending upon the desired outcome, curds can be stirred, kneaded, cut, stacked, or even cooked. The treatment of the curd determines the texture of the cheese: for a soft, fresh cheese, the curd is simply ladled into a perforated mold and allowed to drain. For a cheddar, the curds are stacked into piles that squeeze the whey from the bottom layers, and then are restacked and drained so that each layer has a turn on the bottom. For a cheese with the consistency of mozzarella or provolone, the curd is plunged into hot water and then pulled into thick strands like taffy.

Once the curd has been worked, it is pressed into forms. This is what turns curd to cheese and is so important to the process that the French and Italian words for cheese, *fromage* and *formaggio*, come from the Latin root *forma*, or mold. The sizes and shapes vary, though all cheese forms allow for some method of drainage. For harder cheeses, a weight is placed on the top of the form to press out the last

drops of moisture. When the cheese is sufficiently stiffened to be removed from the form, it is taken out, and, if salt hasn't already been
added to the curds, the cheese is salted.

From this point on, the cheese is in a process of maturation. In
the longer-aging cheeses, this takes place in a cool, dry room where
the cheese may live for years before it emerges onto the market. For
other types, ripening is hastened by the introduction of bacteria,
yeast, or mold, and by curing in a warm or moist space where these
additions can bloom. Depending upon the maker's technique during
a cheese's maturation, possible results can include a soft interior
coated in white down (a bloomy rind), a firm interior within a rind
that's been regularly rubbed with brine (a washed rind), or a dense
creamy block, mottled with blue (a classic blue-veined). In each case,
the conditions must be carefully monitored to ensure that the living
microorganisms that cause ripening neither run amok nor die.

This is where an impassioned Max McCalman enters the picture.
"Cheese is alive," he repeats like a mantra, and he speaks of his role
as twofold; he is both its promoter and its caretaker. When an artisan
has put so much work into a product, in some cases spending years
with a cheese before it is ready for retail sale, Max sees it as his responsibility to tend it through maturity and ensure that it reaches the
table at the exact moment it peaks. And so, as we ask him questions
he continues his daily regimen, appraising every specimen, which
range in size from morsel to slab, and placing them carefully among
the congregation of cheeses on his cart. At times, moved by aesthetic
or gustatory considerations, Max pauses and reconsiders his juxtapo-
sitions, shifting the cheeses like pieces on a chessboard.

Our questions for Max are relatively basic. Sitting in cool humidity among wooden racks of wine bottles, perched on chairs
brought in from the dining room, we ask Max who are America's
premier artisanal goat-cheese makers.

"Judy Schad, of course, Laura Chenel, Mary Keehn," Max lists these cheese-world celebrities in an offhand manner, and we're too embarrassed by our ignorance to ask for repetition. I take notes frantically, phonetically spelling unfamiliar names. His voice is lost in a rush of air as he opens the glass doors of the cave, and he continues to call out names, though he might as well be in a wind tunnel.

"Is the recorder getting any of this?" I mouth to Karl, who grimaces and shrugs. I continue scribbling on my notepad.

When Max ducks out of the cave and returns to the cart, we ask him where these people are and what types of goat cheese they're making.

"In truth, most American goat cheese comes from California, but there is superb cheese coming out of dairies in Indiana, Alabama, and Texas. The people who are doing it right understand goat's milk— they know that it doesn't make a giving or forgiving cheese. Cheese is a living thing, and goat cheese, especially, needs to breathe while it ages." A coating of ash, Max thinks, makes a perfectly sufficient rind.

"What I like to see are cheese makers who eat their own cheeses," he continues, and his praise generally goes to those who have done exhaustive research before embarking on their enterprise. (Karl and I exchange a self-congratulatory glance.) He stresses the importance of the French concept of *terroir*, a term that literally means a foodstuff's provenance, but more broadly means both the land and the culture from which it comes. His biggest piece of advice to a budding cheese maker is this: taste what the Europeans have made and use it as your standard.

Where Max really becomes excited—setting down his cheese to gesture, raising his voice from the modulated tones that for so much of our interview have trailed off into the cave—is in discussing the differences between European and American cheese makers, and especially the trials of the Americans. The issues that affect them are numerous. European subsidies of artisanal cheese makers drive down the prices of imports and, perversely, make domestically produced cheeses more expensive in America than those produced in France. Raw-milk legislation—the statutes demanding that most milk sold in the United States be pasteurized—makes Max nearly apoplectic: "It's alive. You pasteurize it and it's dead. You kill it, *you kill it*." He sighs, "Would you rather eat live food or dead food? Live." The question is rhetorical, but Karl and I find ourselves silently answering, "Live, of course, live." This legislation, which in the past dealt mostly with cow's milk, has begun to take a broader view, encompassing all types of dairy and exposing goat's milk producers to much more stringent regulation.

But the most difficult issues, hands down, are the public misconceptions about goat's milk cheeses. When Max arranges a cheese plate for restaurant patrons, he says, he routinely asks them if they have any preferences. The most common answer, whether they like creamy Camemberts or stinky blues, is that they would prefer that their plate include no goat cheese. The true reason for this is a mystery, though Max has some theories. The first is fear; for many American restaurant goers, the introduction of a cheese course is itself relatively new. The variety of cheeses that to a connoisseur is thrilling, is to the uninitiated a little nervous-making. With so many possibilities, the chance to weed out anything, and in the process assert some control, is perhaps attractive. But why weed the goat? The most likely reason is a simple ignorance of the glorious possibilities of goat's milk cheeses.

To those in the know, the term *goat cheese* encompasses a delightfully broad spectrum with seemingly endless variety. Goat's milk can be made into a cheese that's sweetly marbled and blue; another that's salty, dense, and dry; even one that's moist and springy on the tongue. The cheeses that Karl and I found on our early dairy expeditions just skimmed the surface of what's available; goat cheese can signify practically anything. The animal from which milk comes does little to determine the type or texture of cheese that can be produced. Though it may be influenced by characteristics of the milk, the style of cheese is ultimately decided by choices made by the cheese maker during production.

To many, however, the process of cheese making remains a mystery, and goat cheese means only one thing: chalky white logs of fresh chèvre. They imagine something bland, unworthy of their cheese plate, or worse, are overpowered by the fear of a cheese so goaty that it smothers a fine meal's lingering glow with a distinctly barnyard film. Max would like to educate these people, to encourage them to broaden their palates, but they don't cause him to lose sleep.

That honor is reserved for another group whose abstention from goat cheese really, well, gets Max's goat. It's pregnant women for whom goat cheese has been classed in the same forbidden category as raw oysters and hard liquor. Max scoffs at this prohibition, citing his own family as evidence. While pregnant with their daughter, Max's wife consumed raw-milk goat cheeses with no ill effects.

The reason for abstention, according to the medical community, is that soft, fresh cheeses are more susceptible to the bacterium *Listeria monocytogenes*, commonly called *Listeria*, which causes the infection listeriosis in humans. To a healthy adult, listeriosis produces mild flulike symptoms, but to a pregnant woman, it can cause premature delivery, stillbirth, or an infection in the fetus. It's a serious concern, especially because pregnant women are twenty times more likely to get listeriosis than other healthy adults.

The focus on goat cheese as a carrier, however, is less clear. *Listeria* lives in soil and water. Animals can carry it without seeming ill, and vegetables can become contaminated with it through the soil. Any raw or unpasteurized food has the potential for contamination.

Pregnant women are not routinely advised to avoid salad bars or raw vegetables, though they are both prime potential breeding grounds for the bacterium. Yet Googling "goat cheese pregnancy" turns up dozens of entries citing "Foods to Avoid While Pregnant," and, in one particularly dire warning, advises that indulging in a wedge of goat cheese while pregnant may cause "your baby to get sick or die." Listeriosis is of course a serious concern, but these notices play on every pregnant woman's fear, infusing the cheese with guilt.

Max is right to be concerned about the influence that these kinds of articles have on the cheese-eating public. As in most cases, the truth is much less sensational than we're led to believe. Yes, raw milk, like unwashed vegetables and undercooked meat, carries a greater risk of bacterial contamination. But as with any dairy product that is sold legally in the United States, goat's milk cheeses must either be pasteurized or, if made with raw milk, they must be aged more than sixty days. The cheeses must also be made by a licensed cheese maker in a certified dairy, and the facility must be available for testing by health inspectors and USDA officials. In terms of public safety, Max asserts, goat's milk cheeses pose no more of a risk than any other dairy product. In terms of taste, they are incomparable.

As our interview winds to a close, we ask Max how he would assemble an all–goat cheese plate. In response, he puts one together for us, pairing it with complementary wines and apologetically sending us to a banquette near the bar as the first of the evening's diners trickle to reserved tables in the main dining room. Aesthetically, the plate is lovely—four small wedges of cheese set in a pinwheel around a mound of sliced fig and almond cake, prune and walnut cake, a domino of the Spanish quince paste *membrillo*, and two Medjool dates. The cheeses are arranged clockwise in the order in which they are to be eaten. Beginning with the mildest and most delicate, Chabichou du Poitou, the flavors become progressively stronger with the hearty Mont St. Francis, the edgy Ibores, and the final tingling Harbourne Blue. Max sends us glasses of Pouilly-Fumé to accompany the first three, and he pairs a sweet Quart-de-Chaume with the blue.

There are no crackers; this is pure, unadulterated cheese. We make our way around the plate, cutting thin slivers and nibbling them first alone, then with the wine, then with the accompaniments. The Chabichou du Poitou, a soft, almond-colored stripe of rind wrapping around a slice of blinding white, tastes fresh and mildly goaty, its texture creamy on the tongue. Arresting us with a penetrating, almost meaty scent, the raw-milk Mont St. Francis is firm and rimmed in a thin russet (the rind, Max tells us, is washed, though at the time this means nothing to us). The paste of the Spanish Ibores is ivory, but its rind is a vivid, almost orange color—while it ages, it's rubbed with olive oil and sweet paprika. The cheese is dense and goaty on our palates, and though I know nothing of its history, I immediately think of it as a "worker's" cheese. The marbled Harbourne Blue, last on the plate, is redolent in our nostrils, but in the mouth it transforms to a creamy sweetness. Even Karl, who in the past has generally avoided blue cheeses, is amazed; his eyes open wide as he rolls some on his tongue, "Wow, this is great!"

Giving the cheese our total attention, we try to dissect each flavor, noting with astonishment how much it changes depending on the wine or bit of fruit that follows. With a sip of bright, cleanly perfumed Pouilly-Fumé, each cheese is sharpened on our palates, presenting its flavors at their strongest. The sweeter Quart-de-Chaume, in contrast, reveals subtle, hidden elements in the mellower cheeses—nutty, buttery aftertastes, a breathy hint of musk—while the fruit softens the pungency of the blue. On its own, the sweet, grainy bite of *membrillo* is a revelation, but in harmony with the Ibores, it is nearly holy.

Although we had considered ourselves foodies, this is the first time that either of us has focused our palates with such concentrated intensity. The cheeses seem to release a new flavor with every breath we take, and their superb complexity is completely new to us. It is as though we are just learning to taste.

Leaving Picholine, we feel somehow more civilized and certainly better educated. Back in the muggy dusk of an August evening, we think of Max in the cool with his cheeses, spending his working life tending them with total devotion and, in his words, "spreading the curd" to others. His passion makes sense to us in a new way, and feeling as if we've received his blessing, we prepare to go forth with his missionary zeal.

Chapter 2

A few days later, after simultaneously celebrating our final days of employment and enduring the Great Northeast Blackout, we take a break from packing up the apartment to visit the country house of a friend in West Exeter, New York. The area had once been home to dozens of dairy farms, but now agriculture is interspersed with vacationers, and the closest many get to a working farm is the living history museum in Cooperstown, where we buy horehound candy and watch a docent spin linen from flax. As cottony white tufts drift overhead in a bright blue sky, we drive through rolling emerald hills, breathing the deep smells of late summer and feeling alive.

Our friend Ames, whom we are visiting, doesn't have many neighbors or know the ones he does, but when we arrive, he greets us with cheese and tells us he's discovered a goat farm not a mile down the road. He suggests we visit the next afternoon.

At this point, the goat project is still pretty amorphous. We've quit our jobs, broken our lease, and told all our friends that we have big news. At that, most of them, like my former roommate, look both expectant and smug.

"Karl and I," I begin, watching the complacent smile spread. I take a breath before continuing, "are leaving New York to drive around the country interviewing goat farmers!"

At that point in the conversation, the eyes begin to look confused, the brow furrows, the mouth opens. "That is not *at all* what I thought you were going to say," each friend confesses. "I thought you had gotten engaged."

I'll admit that I love this moment. Defying people's expectations to follow our offbeat dream makes me feel fantastic about myself and Karl and our relationship. It feels like the whole world is before us, ripe with possibility.

This feeling is bolstered by the fact that most people, when their initial shock has passed, have a goat story of their own to share. Hip, young New Yorkers regale us with tales of escaped pet goats, beer-drinking goat mayors, and an itinerant herder, "The Goat Man," who lived on the outskirts of Ashland, Oregon. With every story, we become more anxious to follow the herd.

The practical considerations, a methodology of sorts, have yet to be determined. We haven't figured out the etiquette that will later govern our project—will we map it out in advance? Stab blindly at the atlas? Surf from sofa to sofa? We have no idea.

We've also never spent any time with goats.

"What if we don't like them?" I agonize to Karl, "What if all the stereotypes are true and they stink and they're randy and we don't connect with them at all?"

"Then we've made a huge mistake."

The next day, on our way to Skyland Farms, we wonder if showing up unannounced will be awkward and off-putting to the proprietors.

"Is this rude?" I ask Karl, inexplicably nervous, "Can we really just arrive on someone's doorstep and ask for a tour?" We're not formal people, but we do prefer a sense of protocol. (Our eventual system, it turns out, will not be much different than it is for this visit. While usually we'll precede a visit with a phone call or e-mail, our basic modus operandi will be to show up, wander around, and ask questions.)

Pulling our compact rental car into a small, rutted lot, we are dwarfed by farm equipment on either side but manage to attract the attention of Dave Bernier, former Army Ranger and current goat farmer. Dave is a gregarious and robust man—at any moment, I half expect him to clench up and ask us to punch his stomach—and he seems genuinely pleased that we're interested in his goats.

"Are you Tim and Colleen?" he asks. When we answer no, he tells us that he's actually expecting another couple, Tim and Colleen Avazian, pig farmers from far upstate who are thinking of starting a goat operation. We're just in time for a tour.

The goats at Skyland Farms are Boer goats, a breed that was developed in South Africa where its meat is a staple of the local diet. Dave tells us that Boers are the Black Angus of goats, muscled and meaty, with a frame that supports a high rump and a broad chest. They are bred not for milking, but for bulk, with solid, rounded bones that support their stocky build. Unlike dairy breeds, which in America are dehorned (or disbudded, as it's called in the goat world) at birth for later ease of milking, Boer's horns are left intact, short and close to the head. Like so much about them, their noses are massive, convex, and somewhat Roman in appearance. Their long ears sometimes hang past the chin. In coloring, they're generally white and a kind of chestnut red; from a distance, a friend of ours described a herd of Boer goats as looking like "a bunch of Jack Russell terriers."

The word *Boer* means "farmer" in Afrikaans, the language spoken among white South Africans of Dutch ancestry. A *Boer bok* simply means farm goat, a name meant to distinguish it from the Angora goats that were imported to South Africa from central Asia in the mid-nineteenth century. The Boer as we know it today emerged in the early twentieth century, as farmers began breeding goats for meat.

Federal law in the United States makes the direct importation of livestock from Africa almost impossible, but in 1991, Boer embryos were brought to Canada where they were implanted in Canadian goats and then introduced to the United States. The goats were originally sold at exotic animal shows, where the first Boers in America fetched prices as high as $60,000 each. In the years since, pureblooded Boers have been crossed with Nubian goats, a dairy breed with similar features, to create "percentage" animals. Over time, provided they're bred with other Boers, their lineage is well documented, and they conform to breed standards, the offspring of percentage animals can be considered pure enough for registration, which significantly increases their value.

Dave tells us that he got into Boers in 1994 after raising pigs and, for a short while, dairy goats. He's an active member of the American Boer Goat Association and is firmly convinced that Boers are the livestock of the future. What he loves about them, he explains to us, "is the freedom." The animals themselves are clean and relatively low maintenance, and the business of raising animals for meat, unlike a dairy, is not heavily regulated. By selling live breeding stock to farmers like the Avazians—who have arrived and are walking through the barns with us—and fresh goat meat and sausage at the local farmers' markets, Dave assures us that his animals pay for themselves. ("How do you choose which goats to slaughter?" we ask, and Dave shrugs: "Whoever's slowest.") Since the Berniers send their goats to a local slaughterhouse for butchering, they're not under constant monitoring by an inspector from the Food and Drug Administration; as long as they keep their paperwork up to date and have demonstrably healthy animals, the Berniers are free to raise their goats in whatever manner they choose.

At Skyland Farms, this means vast green pastures occupied by hundreds of goats and a handful of guard llamas and enormous white Maremma dogs. On this warm afternoon, the goats wander as they please. The does and their kids laze in the sun, caper on rolls of hay, and stare curiously at the strangers in their field. Occasionally a kid hops in a capriole, twisting its back and clicking its hooves together as it springs through the air. Following Dave through the barn and into a field, a friendly Nubian doe—a holdover from the Berniers' cheese-making experience—comes up to nuzzle us.

Beyond the barn, we pass a group of pens where bucks are confined separately. Dave lets them in with the general population only at intervals so that he can track each new baby goat's parentage. In their pens, the bucks chew their cud and occasionally bend down their heads to urinate in their beards, a habit that is meant to attract female goats and contributes to their strong scent. The smell of freshly mown grass is heavy on the breeze; across the road, local farmers are helping to cut and bale hay in one of Dave's fields. Calling to us from their farmhouse, his wife comes up with a tray of just-baked chocolate and mint cookies.

We are in love with the afternoon, and it's a good thing. In our first true interaction with goats, our fears are allayed. We like them. We like them very much. Wandering off from our human herd, we mingle with the animals, squatting to scratch their wide bellies, leaning in and laughing when they nibble on my notepad and Karl's camera strap. Their hair is softer than we expect, and away from the bucks, the does smell sweetly of their cud. Deep in the pasture, we see a kid nursing at its mother's teats. Closer to us, Colleen Avazian has also wandered into the herd and is down on all fours, playing with a young goat. The animals are friendly and entertaining, curious, and as interested in us as we are in them. We've made the right decision; we're ready for more.

As goats rub their snouts against our pant legs, Karl and I hold hands and are in our own pastoral dream, where our feet sink into the earth, and the sun, filtered through a bank of trees, is golden.

Chapter 3

Back in the city, Karl and I spend a day in Chinatown, scouring
the storefronts and stalls of street vendors for goat parapher-
nalia. It's the Chinese Year of the Goat, a fact that seemed like
a cosmic sign and a favorable omen when we were first considering
Dr. Fraum's advice. At this point it's August and although New Year's
celebrations are about six months past, between faux pashmina
shawls and Rolex knockoffs we find a surprising number of goat-
themed goods: sticky window decals of goats in New Year's dress, red
and gold currency envelopes emblazoned with horned heads, some
greeting cards and figurines. Over dim sum with our friend Bret, a
balding, bespectacled food writer who has won George Costanza
look-alike contests, is a graduate of the Cordon Bleu, and an unlikely
speaker of fluent Mandarin, we ask about the role of goats in China.

"In Chinese," he explains, gesturing with deftly held chopsticks,
"there's one character that can mean either *goat* or *sheep*. Sometimes
the zodiac is interpreted as a goat, other times as a sheep."

But which is it? His recollection of the livestock he encountered while living in China doesn't include goats along the lines of the dairy animals he'd seen in France, but they weren't quite sheep, either.

"For you two, let's call the animal a goat." Bret continues, "In the Chinese zodiac, it's considered a patron of the arts and its year is supposed to be one of harmony and creativity and travel." He gives us a benevolent smile.

We suspect that he might be making some of this up, but Bret insists it's true. Horoscopes aside, he writes the Chinese character for goat on a napkin, which I tuck carefully into my wallet.

We leave New York at the end of August. Piling Godfrey and all our possessions into a U-Haul, we drive to Maine, where Karl's parents are letting us store our things at their lake house. We're also living with them for much of the fall, dog-sitting while they're on a three-week vacation and then staying on through the Jewish High Holidays.

Their house is right on the lake, looking out on an expanse of water dotted with pine-covered islands. (Across the way is a summer camp, and when Karl was a camper, his parents dropped him off by boat.) At night, you can hear the neighbors' conversations and over them, the pealing call of the loons. We relax to the lapping of the water; having been here before for long summer weekends, it's easy to forget that we're not simply on vacation.

On our first night in Maine, we have dinner on the wide porch with Karl's parents, his dad at the grill, his mom tossing a salad. Before we eat, Karl's father raises his glass and delivers a long, rambling toast about new beginnings and taking risks, ending with a charge to "Goat get 'em!"

After salad, the questions begin. "So how long are you going to be on this trip?" Karl's mom, Nancy, asks.

"We're not really considering it a trip," I say, "It's more of a research project . . . to see if goat farming is something we really want to do."

"And what will you do for money?" Bruce, Karl's dad, a retired accountant, cuts to the chase.

"Well, we had some T-shirts printed up and we're going to sell them," Karl starts, "and Margaret is making hand puppets that we'll also sell through the Web site."

Bruce squints and looks skeptical. He turns to me, "Have you ever made a goat puppet before? Are you working from a pattern?"

"No," I admit, feeling a little less confident in our plan. "But I've made a lot of hand puppets before . . . it can't be that hard." In the U-Haul, the plan had seemed brilliant.

"Hmm," Bruce says in an undertone, "Sort of like the 'Button Hut.'" His enthusiasm for our project has turned to fatherly concern. We assure him that we'll also be doing freelance work from the road, but while he's externally supportive, we can tell that he has serious doubts. After an awkward silence, the four of us spend the rest of dinner talking about their vacation plans.

Later, Karl tells me that the Button Hut was a button-making business he set up with his sister when he was nine. Though ultimately our puppets, made of bright fleece with real mohair beards, bring in a respectable total of $1,000, when averaged out over the time spent on each—close to ten hours—the hourly rate is embarrassingly low. Later in the year when we're staying in my mother's house in Wichita and orders have backed up, we start referring to her dining room as the "puppet sweatshop." Sadly, I think the Button Hut may have been the more lucrative enterprise.

Our travel plan at this point is unformed. We intend to visit as many states as possible and to see goats in a variety of situations, but we also want to allow our project to develop organically. It's an adventure, a goat odyssey, and though there are certain events we know we cannot miss, we want to leave as much room for serendipity as possible. While we're based in Maine, we're tackling the East

Coast; in the spring while we're house-sitting in Kansas, we'll explore the West.

Since so many of the artisanal products we found in New York came from farms in New England, we anticipate a fall full of cheese. Our preliminary research turns up dozens of cheese makers in the region, making everything from fresh chèvre to goat Camembert to biting, striated blues. Caitlin Hunter, goat owner, award-winning cheese maker, proprietor of Appleton Creamery, and president of the Maine Cheese Guild, gives us names of guild members and suggestions of whom to contact. Visits to the local fairs give us an idea of the extent of the growing role of goats in New England. In particular, Paul Hopkins, goat superintendent of Maine's Fryeburg Fair, guides us through his twenty-five-year history in the goat world and explains the growing acceptance of the animals at a fair that has traditionally been dominated by cattle, pigs, and poultry. There's been so much interest that this year, he tells us, the fair organizers had to limit the number of participating goat farms. What's changed about the goats? "The quality of the livestock has just improved enormously," he tells us, "It's taken a quantum leap."

Using Caitlin's and Paul's recommendations as a guide, we look for goats in every place that seems likely: fairs, farms, and cheese counters. We find them almost everywhere. One day at the local Hannaford Bros. grocery store, however, we're surprised to see goat in the meat department. There, in the freezer case, are cuts of goat meat, arranged neatly and marked with handwritten labels.

Since 2001, south-central Maine has been home to a growing population of Somali immigrants. Living primarily in the larger cities of Portland and Lewiston/Auburn, the Somalis are for the most part Muslim, and like many new arrivals to the United States, live in a close, somewhat segregated community. Coming from a warm, agrarian background, the cities of Maine—with their seasons and lobsters and Bean boots—must come as a tremendous shock. Carrying goat meat at the grocery store, a manager tells us, is one way that the community is reaching out to them.

In the weeks before Ramadan, we discover another type of outreach: a livestock auction that has been organized by the state's extension service to unite Somalis with local goat and sheep producers. Anticipating that many families will want a whole animal to slaughter according to the rules of halal for the festival, extension agents have partnered with a Muslim professor from the University of Maine at Orono, who is certified to oversee halal slaughters. They have invited local farmers and local Muslims, putting out the word through farm co-ops and mosques and posting Xeroxed notices around the state.

The leaves are beginning to turn as Karl and I drive the winding roads to a small town in north-central Maine. The drive is beautiful, the epitome of quaint New England: clapboard houses, distant church spires, a few rosy streaks left of dawn. Having been neither to livestock auctions nor halal slaughters before, we have no idea what to expect. Pulling into the auction house lot, there are fewer cars than we anticipated, though several trucks with attached trailers are parked around the side of the building. Indoors, a woman in a glass booth asks if we plan to bid (if so, there is a form to fill out) and then directs us to the auction ring around back.

Many people are milling around, but we see very few who appear conspicuously Muslim, and only one man of African descent. Walking around the pens behind the auction ring, we are looking at the goats when we meet the sole representative of the Somali sacred community, a cleric named Talib Islam. Tall and well built, he wears a knit cap, flannel shirt, jeans, and rubber boots, and could easily have been mistaken for one of the farmhands helping with the animals. He is clean shaven, with bright blue eyes and a laconic Texas drawl. Touching his heart, he greets us with "Salaam aleikum."

Talib Islam was born Taylor Botts on a fourth-generation goat farm in Rock Springs, Texas. Raised a Baptist, Talib converted to

Islam in his early twenties, adopting a new name and becoming the Imam of a mosque in Austin before eventually leading a mosque in Lewiston, Maine. Following the attacks on September 11, Talib and his family received death threats, and his mosque came under investigation. Though his records and computers were seized, he was never charged with a crime. Feeling under suspicion—"I was just plain scared for my family"—he was no longer comfortable in the community, so he shaved his beard, began to dress like a farmer, and moved his family to the country. He shows us his driver's license, where he's pictured with a full beard and a white skullcap, and asks us, "Can you believe that's me?" He remains an observant Muslim and continues to work with the Islamic Somali community, but he no longer lives within it. Now, he's an intentionally difficult man to reach; pulling out his cell phone, he tells us that only his family has this number. For everyone else, there's the U.S. postal service. In the country, he raises animals and is a certified halal butcher; today, he's checking out the auction for the Somalis.

There are many factors that have kept the Somalis away, and Talib ticks them off on his fingers like a checklist. The first is distance; the auction is held early in the morning in East Corinth, Maine, a town one hundred miles north of Lewiston. (Karl and I, starting thirty miles closer, had left the house at six to arrive on time.) Assuming that they had transportation and a trailer that would accommodate livestock, round-trip, the drive alone would take upwards of four hours.

The second factor is cultural. In the Somali community, women generally do the household shopping; selecting appropriate, *zabiha* (unblemished) animals for the holiday is a task that would fall to them. This sale is being held at Tilton's Auction House and is arranged simply as an American livestock auction; a speed-talking caller announces the animals as they are herded into the sawdust ring. Patrons of both genders sit on tiered concrete steps, clustering in the middle for the best view. To attract the attention of the spotters who watch the audience for bids, a potential buyer needs to make eye contact, raise a hand, or generally give a physical signal. Assuming that a recent Somali immigrant could decipher the caller's announcements and figure out the system, she would then have to make a display of herself, something that the rules of modesty would not allow.

The final and most overwhelming obstacle is the general scarcity of zabiha animals for sale. For an animal to be considered appropriate for halal slaughter, it must be completely intact: in demonstrably good health, horns left on and unbroken, testicles in place. If it is female, it must not be pregnant. Either the extension agents have not passed this information along, or the farmers have disregarded it. Gesturing to the animals in the pens and those on their way to the ring, Talib says, "Take a good look at these goats." It's clear even to us that very few of them meet these specifications. He gives us a significant look, both incredulous and disappointed.

A recent newspaper article had noted that the Somali community imports more than $300,000 worth of goat meat to the state of Maine each year. Until earlier in the week, Talib explains, the Somalis had planned to attend, but the three prohibitive factors had finally outweighed the attractions of the sale. Talib has come to observe and report back to the community leaders, but by midmorning he is unimpressed. Not only would the auction have been awkward, he concludes, but it verged on insulting; the disregard of Somali cultural norms was just too much. In spite of this, he's concerned about the impact that their absence will have on the image of Somalis in the state. Though he feels that they are right to stay away, Talib worries that the backlash of public opinion will fall on the Somali community, that the Somalis will seem uncooperative and ungrateful, and that the state will give up the attempt to connect with them. "They were very open-minded," Talib tells us of the Somalis, "But it just wasn't the right situation."

What, we wonder, would be the right situation? Talib suggests that one-on-one connections—farmers selling directly to the community—has the most potential. The idea resonates with us; by taking the exchange to such a small scale, communication would necessarily improve. Our fantasies immediately spiral into a full-blown cultural dialogue, facilitated by goats. Imagining ourselves on a farm, we picture the Somali community coming to visit, buying our goats, Muslims and Jews working together. We file away the idea.

Though there are few, some members of Maine's Muslim community have come to the auction, notably a group of graduate students from the nearby University of Maine in Orono. Studying everything from chemistry to political science, the men have come to America from the Middle East and North Africa to continue their education. In general they're a worldly group, clearly from their respective country's educated elite. None were trained in animal slaughter—they are academics, not butchers—but all agree that no matter how devout they are the rest of the year, as Muslims it is both their duty and their honor to sacrifice an animal for the holiday. Between them they buy fourteen goats and sheep, and one young man who notices us taking notes and photos asks if we'd like to accompany them to the slaughter.

The extension service has arranged for the use of a USDA-certified facility, but when the group of us arrives, we're told that because of the manner in which the animals will be killed, federal law requires that the actual slaughters take place outside. At around noon, in a dusty field behind a large work shed, the graduate students spread out a rubber mat, and with a great metallic scrape, begin sharpening knives.

Karl moves around the mat taking pictures, but I remain on the periphery, the only woman in the field. Aziz, a young chemistry student from Morocco with a shaved head and an athlete's build, is standing next to me and explains the ritual. In order for a slaughter to be considered halal, the animal must be facing east (toward Mecca) when it is killed. A prayer of gratitude and thanksgiving is recited as its throat is slit with one deft stroke. Once dead, it is bled completely, and before any other animals can be brought into the area, all traces of the slaughter must be cleaned. "The most important part," he says, "Is that the animal be calm." It must have no idea of its fate.

Aziz has never slaughtered an animal before—at home in the Atlas Mountains the honor has always fallen to his father—but his grandfather was a halal butcher, and he has witnessed the ritual many times. Nevertheless, he is reluctant to participate. "I know that I should," he tells me, "I am a practicing Muslim, it is my duty." Yet he visibly cringes as each animal is led to the mat. I cringe, too, hearing the nervous laughter and watching the difficulty with which the men subdue the animals, the struggle, the last convulsive shudders. Over the goat, one of the other students says something in Arabic, and I ask Aziz to translate.

"He is thanking the animal for giving its life, and, *bismillah allah o akbar*, saying a prayer to thank Allah," he translates in a low voice, turning to look at me rather than facing the slaughter. Throughout, Aziz stands near me, critiquing the techniques of others, but does not take part until the end when the others are exhausted and strained. Stepping to the mat, he looks tremendously sad.

I admire this respect for the animal. Once their initial self-consciousness has passed, all of the men are grave as they hose down the mat and rinse their knives, tagging each carcass for their respective families, wiping their hands and preparing to go. They seem serious in a way that I hadn't expected; a pervasive solemnity hovers, as though we've just attended a funeral or performed a sacrament, which in a way we have.

Unlike our afternoon with Dave Bernier, where Karl and I were caught up in the romance of the fields and death seemed distant and incidental, on this afternoon we have watched the transformation of these animals from living creatures to cuts of meat. The closeness we've witnessed between life and death disturbs us. On our way home, we talk about that suspended moment of the last breath, that instant when life is snuffed. More than the sticky crimson of blood, or the twitches that were clearly involuntary muscular spasms, it is that instant of choice that disturbs us. No matter how gratefully and gently the goats were killed, it is hard to imagine ourselves making the decision to end a life.

We talk about this reluctance for days. In one jarring afternoon, we have realized that the care and management of livestock includes choosing when life will end. An extension officer I'd spoken with at the auction told me that it was the farming lifestyle and not the individual animals that kept him at it. Though I try to think in those large terms, the greater part of me doubts whether I am capable of that kind of detachment.

It's around this time that we meet Wendy Pieh and Peter Goth. Wendy is a former state legislator who, like me, came from the Great Plains to an eastern women's college and stayed. Peter, originally from a Kentucky horse farm, is a practicing emergency room doctor in midcoast Maine. The couple met while climbing Mount Kilimanjaro, and though neither had ties to the state, they eventually decided to settle in Maine. Over the past fifteen years, they've accumulated two hundred acres of rocky coastal land, which they're "farming by erasure": using goats to remove the underbrush and clearing trees to create pasture. Their Springtide Farm in Bremen is home to about sixty gray cashmere goats, three donkeys, several Great Pyrenees guard dogs, and a stable of black Morgan horses, which Peter trains in teams.

We spend an afternoon with them, walking around their property—their bucks live in a spectacular field overlooking the ocean—and taking turns riding in Peter's horse cart. We immediately feel that they are kindred spirits—active, educated people who have come to goats and agriculture after lives that have taken them all kinds of directions. Though we don't know them well, we trust them.

Sitting over beers and popcorn at their wide wooden kitchen table, we talk to them about the decisions they make as farmers. Their philosophy is one of respect; they treat their animals as humanely as possible, and they make it a priority that their deaths are swift and tranquil. They don't sell live animals for slaughter, but rather the two of them accompany their goats and hold them while they're killed. Wendy openly admits that it's wrenching, but "every tear we shed is one that they don't." Once it's butchered, each goat's meat is marked in their freezer by name.

Wendy and Peter are thoughtful people, and they believe in gratitude. If we are to care for animals, we are responsible for every aspect of their lives, from birth to a comfortable existence to as painless a death as possible. If we are to eat meat, we must decide when that death will come. Their niece, they tell us, is a vegetarian 99 percent of the time but will eat the meat raised on Wendy and Peter's farm because she knows that its existence was the best possible, and its slaughter was performed with respect.

The morality of this approach makes sense to us—rather than distancing ourselves from the individual animals, it requires an even closer engagement, and in its wake, the kind of quiet grief that we observed at the halal slaughter. Though still unsure of our own threshold, we can imagine ourselves adopting this code.

Before we leave their farm, Wendy gives us some links of homemade goat kielbasa, wrapped in butcher paper and mercifully unnamed. We've not yet tasted goat meat, and the next evening, we boil some potatoes and fry the sausage for dinner. Splitting its casings as it sizzles in the pan, it browns quickly and smells of garlic; the kitchen is infused with a vaguely Old World perfume. A lean red meat, the sausage has an earthy flavor similar to strong mutton and though our first few bites are tentative, we quickly lose our inhibitions and enjoy the meal. Pleasure, I suppose, is its own tribute.

Chapter 4

W

e don't buy the Hyundai Santa Fe that will become "the Goat Mobile" until late fall. Until then, for all of our goat adventures, we borrow Karl's mother's car: a tame, white sedan with the surprising license plate KEGEL. To those in her community who know Nancy Schatz as a Lamaze teacher and a local pioneer in natural childbirth, this license plate makes perfect sense. To truckers on I-95 who see me driving, Karl asleep in the passenger's seat, Godfrey poking his head out of a rear window, it does not. Cruising along, I often forget about the vanity plate, simply enjoying the feeling of driving. And then I remember KEGEL, and I am mortified by the thought that people on the highway are reading the license plate, looking at me, and associating the two. My cheeks burn at every rest stop.

In mid-September, on a journey that takes us three days, we drive from Maine to Memphis. We're so absorbed in our project—in educating ourselves on the minutia of the goat world—that on the second day of travel, our overnight stop in Manhattan comes as a shock.

Though we've only been gone for a few weeks, we feel as though it's been an eternity. The fact that we're staying with friends, that we have no apartment of our own, accentuates the profound disconnect we feel between ourselves and the city. Walking quietly across Midtown on a misty night after a boisterous dinner of tapas, we're struck by the light beading on greasy asphalt, the warm blasts of air bursting up through the subway grates, the sheer immensity of the buildings. The city, in all its gritty glory, is achingly beautiful. But it is no longer ours.

We drive to Tennessee somewhat haunted by this, feeling acutely as though we no longer belong in New York but with no clear idea of where we are headed. We just know that right now, we're going South.

We're on our way to one of the strangest and most exciting events we'd stumbled upon in our initial goat research: the International Goat Days Family Festival, held annually in Millington, Tennessee, a bedroom community outside Memphis. At once a celebration of goats and an all-American country fair, the festival has only been in existence for a little more than a decade—just since founder Babe Howard decided that he wanted to race goats—but in those years it has become a Tennessee institution. Drawing between six and seven thousand visitors annually, the Goat Days Web site says it now includes costume contests for goats, a Boy Scouts–sponsored goat "pill" flipping contest, milking contests, dairy and meat shows, a goat barbecue cookoff and the "Cabrito Challenge," an Iron Chef-like competition during which contestants are given a few pounds of goat meat and free rein to prepare it as they choose. But the main event is still the goat chariot races.

Encouraged by Silky Sullivan—professional Irishman, goat owner, and man-about-Memphis whose downtown bar boasts an enclosed yard with a small herd of goats and a brick "goat tower"—

Goat Days has become the sister festival of Puck Fair, an eight-hundred-year-old annual celebration of goats in Killorglin, Ireland, to which the organizers of Millington's festival have made several pilgrimages. The word "international" wasn't added to Millington's fair because of this affiliation, however. Goat Days has been global from the beginning when a Mexican team entered the inaugural race and barbecue cookoff.

The festival sounded like a singular opportunity to see goat people at their giddiest and most unguarded, and from the beginning we resolved that no matter the distance between Maine and Tennessee, we'd go to Millington.

Once there we plan to camp at the fairgrounds, and on the advice of a woman we've spoken with in the head office, we arrive before the fair opens, around three in the afternoon, to pitch our tent. (Her fears that we won't find a camping spot if we're late turn out to be completely unfounded; the first night, we go to sleep as the sole campers in the lot and wake to find only one other tent pitched directly next to ours, its owners trying to coax their pet goat out from under their nearby van. Bleary eyed, precaffeinated, I'm convinced that I'm still dreaming.)

Settling in and walking the fairgrounds that first day, we find ourselves in a microcosm of earnest Americana. The whirlwind of the fair begins with a kickoff parade of Scouts, costumed children, Shriners dressed as hillbilly clowns, and a decorated trolley of people who've been brought in from the parking lot, which is now filling with trailers plastered with "Caution: Show Goats" signs. Lasting about five minutes, the procession snakes below the welcome banner, then disintegrates as people find their families and friends inside the grounds. In a wooden corral at the center of the fairgrounds, the Best Dressed Goat Contest follows: small goats squeezed into children's Halloween costumes, large ones saddled and ridden like ponies, and one dressed in a plush cow costume wearing a sign that says "Got Milk?" Karl edges his way into the pen taking pictures and we learn what will be a useful lesson throughout the journey: behind his camera lens, Karl might as well be invisible. With a few notable exceptions (on the killing floor of a slaughterhouse, at the Army-Navy football game), as long as he is holding a camera, Karl can go anywhere.

The winner of the costume contest is Charlie Brown, a pygmy kid dressed as a World War II fighter pilot, complete with leather helmet, flight goggles, cardboard airplane wings, and a white aviator's scarf. He is so small that as he leaves the ring, Charlie Brown's owner scoops him under her arm and carries him through the grounds, pausing only to let me give him a little scratch.

By early evening, past the glut of fair food stalls—funnel cakes, corn dogs, Dutch apple turnovers, and all manner of other fried starches—the barbecue teams have set up their stalls. Under flashing blue lights and the wooden cutout of a pig in sunglasses, the Millington Police Department's "Bad Pigs" barbecue team is preparing for the next day's competition. For a cash donation that will go to local charities, Karl and I load up our plates with shreds of pulled pork and white bread, smoky beans, and puddles of spicy red sauce, breathing in a heady hickory whiff as we make our way down the line. Trophies from past triumphs line the picket fence that marks their stall; superstition has kept them from barbecuing any goat meat today. Gorging ourselves at a picnic table covered in checkered oil cloth, we lick our fingers and overhear the officers discussing tomorrow's strategy while dissecting this evening's barbecue shortcomings. One officer keeps shrugging his shoulders and shaking his head. In a resigned and serious voice, he repeats, "I put 'em on too late, and I'm cookin' 'em slow."

Dusk settles over the fair, and thick violet clouds crowd the evening sky. It looks like a storm is approaching, and the heavy smell of ozone deepens our suspicion. One of the barbecuers tells us it always rains during Goat Days, and when we say we're camping, he just laughs and says merrily, "Well, I sure hope you've got a tarp!" So do we.

The day has been sticky and hot, and in the coolness of the evening we explore the fairgrounds further, stopping at the Boy Scouts' tent where bright orange goat "pills"—dried goat droppings dipped in fluorescent paint—are scattered in a chalked playing field. The object of the game is to flip the pill in a long arc with your thumb, hoping it will land as far into the course as possible. In effect, it's a contest to see who can fling the poop the farthest. For a dollar, Karl tries his hand—tossing the dung an impressive thirty-seven feet on his third try. Unfortunately, he loses by four feet; the winner is a local teenager, whose best flip is forty-one feet.

Closer to our tent on the outskirts of the fairground the goat pens have been set up, and as darkness falls we walk around the baled hay and makeshift grooming parlors that are tucked between pens. Saturday is the main day of the fair, and both dairy and Boer goats will be shown by their owners in competitions that begin early in the morning and stretch until Sunday afternoon.

We've never been to a goat show, but we're expecting something like the Westminster dog shows we've seen on television: obsessive grooming, inflamed passions, a strange language of breed standards that to us is incomprehensible. We can't imagine ourselves showing animals of any kind—Godfrey is a mutt rescued from a shelter and that's the way we like our beasts, hardy and imperfect. But goat shows are a huge part of the goat world, and even people who don't have any desire to display their animals look to the shows when it's time to breed. These are the purest animals, the ones that have been bred for physical perfection. Their traits, we're told, are so engrained that their lineage can be traced from just the curve of their udder or the round of their flank. We're both a little amused—show goats?— and intensely curious.

Our initial guess about the show culture, it turns out, isn't far off; in this last stretch, the goat owners hang painters' lights on the rails of their pens, clipping hair, trimming hooves, and polishing horns well into the night. A cloying floral scent emanates from the chain-link fence that marks the fair's perimeter where a woman shampoos her goats, scrubbing them until they're covered in thick lather, then hosing them down and blowing them dry. Throughout the goat tents, families in matching shirts perform their evening chores; adults and children sleep near the animals on cots in empty stalls. In their pens, the goats rub their horns against the metal bars, grunting and pacing as if in anticipation.

By Saturday morning, any vestige of detached irony that Karl and I have brought with us has completely disappeared. We chat with the elderly women of the Lion's Club Auxiliary at their annual pancake breakfast, admiring the merit badges sewn to their canary-yellow vests. We sit in the stands at the show ring, asking questions of the 4-H leaders as they prepare their kids for the first competitions of the day, which stress the children's showmanship as much as the merits of the animals they lead.

"Just make sure you're making eye contact with the judge," instructs the leader of the Goat Getters from Marion, Kentucky, "and always keep the goat between you and the judge."

It's still early, no later than 7:30, when the kids begin to make their way to the ring. If there is anything more adorable than small, serious children taking charge of livestock, I don't know what it is. Their brows furrowed and their starched white shirts tucked into hand-tooled leather belts, the kids lead their animals by nylon ropes and collars. Their parents and club leaders watch breathlessly from aluminum stands as the goats, with varying degrees of compliance, allow themselves to be displayed. The Goat Getters are well represented, their preparation evident: keeping their eyes on the judge, with their animal always positioned in front of them, they answer with confidence questions about the physiognomy of goats and the diet and history of the particular animal they're showing. Other kids are clearly new to the show ring, hesitating and freezing when their goats act up. Judge Anton Ward, a South African who is one of the foremost Boer judges in the country, assesses each performance, stressing what each child has done well, while giving pointers for the future.

As the morning progresses, the shows become more competitive, with adults replacing the children in the ring and the stakes rising proportionally. Top marks at a goat show can drastically change the value of an animal; the semen of prize bucks commands top dollar, and having a clearly documented, champion-laden lineage ensures that there will be a market if a goat is sold for breeding stock. We had learned some of this from Dave Bernier, but at Millington we see it in action: goat owners maintaining their composure and trying to keep crisp in wilting heat, cajoling their goats, always maintaining eye contact with Judge Ward. The shows continue all day, through the loud booms of the National Championship Anvil Shoot—exactly what it sounds: cannons shooting iron anvils straight into the air—and the long-predicted torrential downpour that forces the judging tent to relocate forty feet to higher ground. Watching it all, Karl and I still can't imagine ourselves out there in the show ring, but we do have a better understanding of the impulse. After the decidedly unglamorous daily regimen of goat care, and years of breeding to achieve certain traits, competitions offer a chance for goat farmers to step into the spotlight for a moment, showing themselves and their animals at their best. The competitions are, we understand, the payoff; no matter how one places, the reward is being in the center of the ring.

On the other side of the fairgrounds, the goat barbecue judging and the goat chariot races are under way. In the barbecue stalls, the teams have been at work since early morning, keeping their coals stoked and their meat evenly dispersed over the grill. Their techniques are as different as their smokers: some teams have clearly invested time and money into the engineering of elaborate drums and portable pits, others seem to depend on their own skills, hovering for hours around rudimentary equipment that requires constant monitoring.

During another sudden and fierce shower, we huddle under the awning of the Trash Cookers, former champions who tell us a few of their secrets. "Most important," they say, "you have to clear the skin of every last hair." Any singed bristles will cause a distinctly goaty flavor. Next in importance is the sauce, but with serious faces they tell us, "We're keeping that secret."

When the competition is over, they offer us a taste of their entry. The meat has been in their drum barbecue for close to eight hours, and in that time has absorbed smoke and spices while melting from the bone and transforming into a tender, moist pile. The long, slow heat has dissolved any sinew or gristle, and the meat fairly glistens as it's unwrapped from its foil. The Trash Cookers fill a paper bowl and point us in the direction of their sauces, lined up in squeeze bottles on the top of a cooler. We use them sparingly, squirting just a spoonful onto the side of the bowl. Karl has the first forkful.

The consistency is similar to pulled pork, shreds of meat softened by the long heat and concentrated with flavor. It's less fatty than pork, and a little gamier, but with a dab of sauce and on its own, the meat holds the essence of barbecue. They must have cleared all the bristles, because there isn't a whiff of goat, just earthy, smoky bites, so soft we barely need to chew them.

It's a little disconcerting to leave the Trash Cookers for the goat chariot races—to eat goat one minute and cheer it on the next. But once the weather clears, the races, which are the heart of this festival, are on. We cross the fairgrounds once more to a makeshift track that has been marked by baled hay near the entrance to the fair where portable bleachers are set in a semicircle at one end. The bleachers are packed with spectators of all kinds, men and women, young and old, country locals and a few conspicuously dressed city folk from Memphis.

The teams cluster around the track, some wearing matching outfits, others in ragtag bands united only by the fact that they're racing together. Karl stakes out the track, and I squeeze into a spot between an elderly couple in coordinated tracksuits and a young family whose kids are playing with a goat marionette. The older man leans over his wife to tell me that the favorites this year are a team from Mexico City. He points the team members out below; they wear matching mustard-yellow Goat Days T-shirts with blue jeans, cowboy boots, and feed caps, and are circling their chariots, tuning them up as though they were race cars. It amazes me that they would travel more than twelve hundred miles to participate in a goat race until I remember that Karl and I have, in fact, traveled sixteen hundred miles to watch them. The man says that the purse this year is $1,000 and nods significantly, as if to explain the Mexicans' trip. I suppose it's a great sum if you're local, but if you're driving a trailer full of goats from Mexico, I can't imagine that it would even be enough to cover gas. There aren't many opportunities for engagement in this esoteric hobby, however, and my guess is that for the devout goat racer, it's not about the money.

Eavesdropping, I find that every conversation is about the same thing: this goat's handicap, that goat's strength, the aerodynamic qualities of various chariots. Meanwhile Karl, with his camera, has managed to find a spot in the middle of the ring; hoping for a photo finish, he's next to the timers.

The competition is run in heats, and each time around the rules are the same: the drivers kneel in their chariots, unable to touch the goats with anything more than a flap of the reins. They can shout and bounce in the chariot, but they can neither touch the goat nor leave the cart. It's like a small-scale reenactment of *Ben-Hur*.

We all lean forward in anticipation as the starting gun sounds. One goat rears majestically, nearly tipping the driver out of his cart. Others start promisingly, taking off from the line with a burst of hooves. Inevitably, it's these front-runners that slow down, and the drivers can be heard giving loud, ineffective "Yeehaws!" and pleading with their animals to "please just keep going!" as the goats get distracted, abruptly stop, or bend to munch on some of the hay marking the course boundary. One goat starts the race at a gallop, continues half a length ahead of the rest of the racers, and then quits just twenty feet shy of the finish line. The crowd hoots, shouts to the goat, and finally collapses in laughter.

I'm wiping tears from my eyes when I find Karl talking to one of the contestants. More than any sporting endeavor we've seen, goat chariot racing seems to be a game of chance. The racer agrees, "Shoot, it's all just luck." No amount of preparation or training or streamlined chariot design could have determined whose goat would win. The favorites—all the way from Mexico City—don't even place.

This year's winner, a man named Kenneth Thompson, tells us that in the 1990s, he was a four-time champion, but for the last four years he's been in something of a slump. After the victory, he admits that he's only been training his goat, Power Stroke, for nine days.

We stay in Millington for another day and a half, but after the goat chariot races, the fair slows down. There are a few more triumphs—Millington's Bad Pigs win the Cabrito Challenge with their Goat Wellington, and a young woman wins the timed juniors milking competition by squeezing a shocking amount of milk into her pail. Doug "The Goat Whisperer" Curle takes home the prize for the year's largest goat competition with Harley, his Nubian wether (a castrated male), which is the size of a Shetland pony.

By the close of the fair, Karl and I are no closer to knowing whether we will truly make it as farmers, but what we do understand more deeply are the tiny glories that sustain so much of America. The local policemen feeding the community, the teenage Boy Scouts tucking in their uniforms to man the pill-flipping booth, the untempered enthusiasm of the 4-H kids for their goats—to us, these are scenes of improbable delight. Through the lens of the goat, we see an America that is in stark contrast to the one we've known. Its scale is small, but its enthusiasm is boundless.

Chapter 5

I n late fall, Karl and I go to Nashville for the American Dairy Goat Association's annual convention. The association—ADGA to the goat world—is the largest and oldest goat organization in the United States. Founded in 1904 and known until the mid-sixties as the American Milk Goat Record Association, ADGA provides both services and a sense of community to goat owners throughout the country. In the age of the Internet, this is especially true, and ADGA hosts Web forums for its members, allowing them to keep up long-distance discussions of the issues affecting them from remote farms in every state.

We learn from its Web site that the organization recognizes six breeds of dairy goats: Alpine, LaMancha, Nubian, Oberhasli, Saanen, and Toggenburg. In the coming years, it will add two more: Sable Saanen and the Nigerian Dwarf. Each has distinctive traits, and though it takes us hours of study, poring over our copy of *Raising Milk Goats Successfully* and quizzing each other in the car as we drive, Karl and I learn to identify them. Alpines are the classic French dairy goat, bred in many colors, that were imported to the United States in the 1920s and are now recognized by the USDA as the goats with the highest average annual milk production. The only breed to originate in the United States, LaManchas also come in a variety of shades and are generally known for their sweet temper; they're easily recognized because they have no ears. Nubians, in contrast, have long ears that frame their faces like lop-eared bunnies, and a broad, convex nose. They're known for producing milk with a high butterfat content.

Then there are the Swiss breeds. Oberhaslis are a deep reddish brown with distinctive black markings on their nose, back, and belly; they are listed as an endangered breed and are not generally included in commercial dairy herds. Saanens and Sable Saanens originated in Switzerland's Saane Valley; Saanens are distinguished by their all-white coats (Sable Saanens are of the same stock but colored). Their milk is considered to be quite good. Toggenburgs, also Swiss, are the oldest registered breed and are identified by their beige coat and white "reverse badger" facial markings.

Nigerian Dwarf goats, which will soon become a registered breed in the United States, are small in stature, of African descent, and were originally introduced in American zoos. Though they don't give quite as much milk as larger goats, what they do produce is exceptionally rich, and some commercial farmers have begun to incorporate them into their herds.

For each breed, ADGA keeps a detailed registry of animals and maintains standards for judging. The group also trains and certifies judges, facilitates the appraisal of goat herds, and sanctions shows throughout the country like the ones we attended in Millington. In addition, an active youth program encourages the next generation of goat farmers. Although it's led by a volunteer board with a relatively small budget, ADGA is responsible for the development of strategies for the general promotion of goats and goat's milk. There's no money for a comprehensive ad campaign like "Got milk?" Here, they piggyback and insert an *A*: T-shirts and bumper stickers read "Goat milk?"

In general, though, the annual convention is a serious event and includes workshops on such diverse issues as cheese making, artificial insemination, disease and parasite control, while providing a yearly opportunity for members from each state's chapters to discuss the association's business in person. It's also a place for dairy goat owners to reconnect with friends and catch up on a year's worth of gossip; when the week coincides with Halloween, as it does this year, it's an opportunity to dust off your favorite goat-themed costume for the final evening's ball.

It's clear when we pull into the parking lot of the Nashville Airport Marriott that this convention is unlike usual hotel events. A large striped tent has been set up at one entrance to the ballroom, and between the cars a few intrepid goat owners walk their animals on leashes. While there's no judged show at the ADGA convention (that's done in July at the ADGA National Show), a champagne brunch and "Spotlight Sale" of juried goats will be held on the final morning, and in the tent prized animals are displayed to potential buyers. Since the convention serves as a meeting place, some members have also brought animals they've sold from a distance, which they house in trailers in the parking lot until they can deliver them to their new owners.

Through the sliding-glass entrance to the hotel, the lobby is dotted with dry erase boards advertising hospitality suites sponsored by various goat clubs, posting changes to the day's schedule of workshops, and serving as a general notepad. We elbow each other and try to suppress giggles when we see that one board reads "Semen Exchange, Room 314."

At a table decorated with bunched balloons, members of the Tennessee Dairy Goat Association, which is hosting the event, register participants and distribute gift bags—canvas totes printed with cartoons of three breeds of dairy goats clustered around a guitar as if singing.

Pinning on our name tags, Karl and I don't know where to begin. We know no one, and a glance at the list of workshops is overwhelming. Though we've been converted philosophically to the goat and have been studying faithfully, the lecture titles are filled with unfamiliar words, technical advice, and discussions of issues that are a mystery to us. Fencing options, caseous lymphadenitis, and the merits of different management techniques all sail by us as we try to formulate our plan of attack. Finally, we decide on a smattering of talks that cover the broadest range of topics—goat reproduction, disease prevention, starting a commercial dairy, marketing, and the cheerfully titled, "Why a Judge Does What He Does." In between, we explore the vendors' area.

In a carpeted hall with accordion partitions, dozens of small businesses have arranged stalls. What they offer varies from practical services to home decor: artificial inseminators, feed and fencing specialists, and tool sharpeners mingle with embroiderers, woodworkers, and goat figurine dealers. Stained-glass goats, novelty T-shirts ("My Nubian is smarter than your honors student"), breed-specific belt buckles, and goat-shaped cookie cutters are interspersed with livestock clippers, milking machine accessories, and semen tanks. (A lucrative sideline in the goat world, we learn, is the collection and sale of semen, which is stored frozen in sealed straws until used for artificial insemination.) This jumble is exactly what the members of ADGA want. As we survey the room, they survey the goods, fingering both practical and frivolous merchandise with enthusiasm.

As with any convention, this one caters to the needs of its participants. There are those with products to sell, those with stories to tell, and those, like us, who want to observe and connect with the greater goat community. Whenever there's a lull—between workshops, after the day's events are complete—Karl and I wander the vendor area, talking with people at their booths.

At a table sprawling with goat objects, we meet Earl and Marge Kitchen of Wood and Stream Creations who have brought with them a selection of goat collectibles from their store, the largest in the country. Marge, with round cheeks and a mop of curly white hair, is almost a caricature of an affectionate grandmother. She shows us paper napkins printed with goats and a wallpaper border of goat-themed toile, and confesses that when she and Earl met almost half a century earlier, they were both showing Labrador retrievers. Now they own Nigerian Dwarf goats. Fingering a porcelain goat figurine painted in Delft blue and white, she invites us to visit them in Minnesota; eventually, we do. As we're walking away from the booth, Karl says, "I just want to hug her."

At another stall, Jim Hershberger, a tall, jovial man in thick glasses and overalls, takes a break from the grinding wheel to tell us that in this one week he sharpens more clippers than he does the rest of the year. We ask him if he owns goats, and he shakes his head, saying that he's on the road too much to keep animals.

Geoff Masterson, of Superior Semen Works, is confident that we'll run into each other again in our travels. His business involves going farm to farm collecting, storing, and selling goat semen. Though he and his wife live in New Hampshire, they spend at least nine months of the year traveling the country in a truck painted with their logo: a mighty sperm, fists raised in victory, within the silhouette of a semen tank. Sitting on a stool next to an enormous stainless steel tank, Geoff unscrews the lid to show us his trade. White clouds of dry-ice smoke billow as he lifts out the straws, holding them with a kind of gentle authority, as carefully as you would unstable fuel rods.

Caprine Supply, the largest dealer of goat supplies in the country and one of the convention's primary sponsors, takes up most of the lobby with its tables of inflation pumps, goat leads, and ear tattoo kits. The proprietors are Joan and Jim Vandergriff, both of whom have owned goats for more than thirty years. Joan, a petite woman with short hair, an irreverent manner, and a surprisingly deep voice, is one of the convention's chairs and offers to introduce us to key board members. Jim, tall, lanky, and bald, a former potter (who, in a strange coincidence, graduated from the same high school I did), tells us that his favorite thing about goats is that they led him to Joan. In addition to being devoted "goaties," they are also devoted bikers, and the two are heading to a motorcycle show after the convention. In the parking lot, they show us the trailer they use to haul their bikes; in a sea of Christian fish symbols, the back of their trailer displays one that reads "Gefilte."

The convention lasts for a full week, but Karl and I are only there for four days. On Wednesday evening, we go to the wine and cheese tasting where we're given wineglasses painted with Purina's red-and-white checkerboard logo—it's another major sponsor of the convention—and heavy, frosted blue plastic plates to hold cheese samples (in the Goat Mobile, these will be our only china for the duration of the year). Long banquet tables in the center of the room are piled with cheese: the ubiquitous fresh chèvres but also cheddars, Goudas, fetas, and a few aged wheels with blooming rinds oozing molten insides where wedges have been cut. Baskets of crackers are strategically placed on the table, as are serving plates heaped with smoked goat sausages.

We sit with a young couple who are just starting out in goats. Like us, they've come to learn everything they can about the animals. Unlike us, they seem captivated by the competitive aspect, determined to breed their goats so that, as the woman tells us with clear determination, "Someday, we'll make it to the national show."

Across the table, a pair of Mexican men with a small cheese operation in Oaxaca have come to taste as many goat cheeses as possible. One has actually apprenticed with a cheese maker in France, but they're curious to see what's being made north of the border. Between them, the men must have twenty pounds of cheese loaded onto their plates, and as they taste each, they smack their tongues against the roof of their mouths, cleanse their palates with bread, jot a few notes in a book that sits on the table between them, and plunge back in. They speak little English, but warmly invite us all to visit them in Mexico.

Karl and I have taken only a modest amount of cheese, some cubes of cheddar and feta, some sliced mozzarella and Gouda, a few wedges of aged goat Camemberts and crottins. We were early in the line when people were delicately spearing their cheese with toothpicks and, in a civilized fashion, sampling just a bit of each. Now, it's become a feeding frenzy. From our table, we turn to look back at the samples where conventioneers are five deep, grabbing at whatever cheese is left on the plates, hotel servers barely able to refill them. It's madness.

The cheese itself varies in quality. ADGA isn't about cheese, really, but about animals, and though some members are making extraordinary cheese, others simply do it to avoid wasting the milk, a by-product of their breeding program. The samples have all been sent in advance, and we overhear people tasting their own cheeses and complaining that it doesn't taste at all like it should, that maybe it "just didn't travel well." Even those attending the convention had to ship their cheese in advance, and no matter how carefully they've packed it, once it arrives at the hotel, there can be no guarantees about how it will be handled. Far from Max McCalman's careful touch and temperature-controlled cave, the hotel's employees may not even know what the package contains.

The cheeses we sample are, for the most part, quite good, with the exception of one bitter cheddar that I actually spit into my napkin. A sweet, milky goat Camembert is especially nice—its texture almost that of condensed milk—and a salty oil-cured feta, flecked with red peppercorns and perfumed with bay leaves, is so perfect that we write down the name on the label, Split Creek Farm. There are hundreds of cheeses, their labels tucked between the array of sample plates, but between us, Karl and I taste fewer than twenty cheeses—the event is simply overwhelming.

The last morning of the conference, Karl and I go to the Spotlight Sale. Run more like an auction of art than one of livestock, the sale is a showcase of promising goats from across the country. Entering the carpeted ballroom, we have trouble finding a seat at the packed tables. Those members who've stayed to attend are serious about their breeding programs and, recovering from the costume ball the night before, lubricated with a little champagne, their bids are high. One man, leaning against the wall near the stage, talks into his cell phone, occasionally flagging a spotter to make sure the auctioneer has seen his bid.

At the corner of a raised dais in the ballroom, an announcer calls out the lineage of each goat, while young does and bucklings are led onto the stage. The handlers are dressed to the nines in black cowboy hats and leather vests, sport coats, and even a tuxedo; the goats are trimmed and polished. With his camera, Karl goes backstage and reports that before they come out, the animals are sprayed with Aqua Net and sprinkled with glitter. From the sidelines, a man with a broom comes out between goats and sweeps their poop from the stage.

Since the animals are young, they are not fully developed, and the announcer emphasizes both their bloodlines and their possibilities. "This is cutting-edge LaMancha breeding, folks," he calls. "Just imagine the mammary system that's gonna be in there!"

The "depth and longevity" of each pedigree is touted, and the bidding, when it begins, escalates to record-breaking figures. Before the sale is over, a young buck of champion stock and forty straws of his semen fetch $16,000.

Throughout the sale, a woman in a pantsuit periodically waves a white handkerchief and hollers, "Yeehaw!" The enthusiasm is contagious, and there's an excitement in the room that's almost palpable, especially as the stakes get higher. The crowd whispers—was the goat really worth that much? Who's the buyer consulting on his cell phone?—and though no verdict is reached, the fun is clearly in the speculation.

It's a little awkward for us, being at a goat convention and sale without actually owning any animals, but by this last morning we understand how people get caught up in this world. The satisfaction of breeding goats for certain traits—creating the perfect udder or stance—must be incredible. The feeling of community at the convention, especially among people whose choice of livestock may elicit raised eyebrows at home, is clear. Though at this point we are outsiders, Karl and I can imagine a day when we'll take part, greeting friends warmly, asking after their animals, feeling connected.

Chapter 6

So much of the goat project hinges upon a vision of ourselves as partners that, in retrospect, it seemed inevitable that as all our New York friends predicted we would decide to get married. When Karl does propose, however, it takes us both completely by surprise.

Between trips to Tennessee, we spend a turbulent afternoon in Maine in late September talking about the trajectory of the project, hashing out our goals and our itinerary. As far as travel goes, Karl is in favor of more structure while I want a looser plan. At the same time, I want to feel as though we have a destination—either physical or intellectual—and that the project will have an end point. We're both used to being adults, working, voting, paying our bills, being responsible members of society, and especially for me, it's jarring to realize that I've chosen to be homeless and completely dependent upon the benevolence of others. About a month out of New York, I'm still glad that we left, but I want to know where in the grand scheme of things we're going. If we ultimately decide that we don't want to be goat farmers, will we also be deciding that we don't want to be together?

Our conversation is heated and long. Eventually night falls, and Karl suggests that we go down to the dock to listen to the loons. It is clear and starry, the lighthouse beacon flashing in the distance. Standing at the water, Karl fumbles with something in his pocket and pulls out a tiny blue box. He turns to me and opens it.

"Will you marry me?" he says, sounding almost as surprised as I am that he's asking. Starting to cry, I nod my head, and finally manage to say, "Yes." He takes my left hand and slides on his grandmother's engagement ring. Amazingly, the fit is perfect.

We set a date for August 8, 2004, and after a quick search, decide to get married in a field overlooking the ocean at a working farm in Maine. Our engagement adds a new dimension to the project—if we do this, we're really doing it together and forever. In some ways, the decision is a relief, but it also adds a whole new set of concerns and choices, many of them frivolous but all demanding attention. There is a caterer to hire, music to arrange, a ceremony to plan. There is a tent to reserve, flowers to choose, invitations to design. I will need a dress. Neither of us wants an elaborate wedding, but we do want something that reflects our personalities and interests—no banquet chicken or seed pearls for us. There's a lot we don't know about the wedding and certainly a lot we don't know about marriage, but as a theme for it all, we choose goats.

Before we left Maine for the ADGA convention, we acquired the Goat Mobile, a small white SUV that will be our home on the road. With the seats down, the back is just long enough for our sleeping bags and just wide enough for the two of us and the dog. On top of the car, we have a long black storage container we call "the Pod," which holds our camping gear and my puppet-making supplies and serves as a traveling billboard; our Web site, www.yearofthegoat.net, is posted in big white letters across the side.

With our own wheels—no more KEGEL!—and our lives together ahead of us, our project begins to feel like an adventure. Our new security in each other makes the insecurity of our situation somehow fun. Whom will we meet? What will we eat? Where will we end up? The possibilities every morning, waking in a motel, a tent, the back of the car, are exciting. The change may be semantic, but it makes all the difference: we're not homeless, we live on the road.

At the end of autumn, after the ADGA convention, we keep heading south. On our way, we decide to see a bit of the country, taking detours to Shenandoah National Park, the Great Smoky Mountains, and the sites of various Civil War battles. We keep an assortment of guidebooks in the car—*Pets on the Go*, *Roadside America*, the incomparable *Roadfood*, which we consult on every highway—and as we drive, we scan them for interesting places to stretch our legs and sample the local flavors. I read entries aloud, suggesting alternate routes so we can eat our way through the region.

"If we take a detour through Nashville, there are homemade peach preserves at the Loveless Café," I say, directing us to plentiful baskets of fresh, pillowy biscuits and dense, chewy steaks of country ham. "If we go through the Indian reservation, it says there are peanuts boiled with ham hocks." (From a cauldron at a roadside stand, we buy a ladleful of boiled peanuts and discover that even though we're Yankees we love the slippery legumes in their soupy broth, the bits of ham floating among the soggy shells.) Even in the sleepiest corners of Appalachia, where gas stations are scarce and cell phone reception nonexistent, we have no trouble finding a hearty, filling, and often surprisingly good meal.

The weather, as we drive, is unseasonably warm. An Indian summer has taken hold of the East, and though it's the middle of November, we camp comfortably, hiking at the end of the day in T-shirts and shorts. The sole drawback, we learn from the cautions of a park ranger at Big South Fork State Park, is that rattlesnakes have reemerged. On our hikes, we hear the phantom rustle of snake tails every time Godfrey darts into the fallen leaves.

Sitting out by our evening fire until long after sundown, organizing our travels, we come up with a rough plan: we'll head to Florida for Thanksgiving at Karl's parents' winter quarters then meander to Kansas to be with my family for Christmas, and from there plan the western legs of our journey. My mother will leave for a spring semester sabbatical in Oregon in January, and while she's gone, her empty house in Wichita will serve as our base, a place with plenty of room to store our accumulated goat materials, do our laundry, and plan our wedding.

The wedding, even in a few short weeks, has taken on a life of its own. Though we'd initially hoped it would be a small, somewhat casual ceremony, it's quickly spinning out of control. Before we left Maine we could see this happening: estimates that at first shocked away our breath ("Eighteen thousand dollars to cater a 'light luncheon?' Are they out of their minds?") slowly began to seem reasonable, customs that initially seemed archaic somehow shifted and became a tradition we needed to preserve, brunches and dinners sprouted into a long weekend of festivity.

From the comfort of Karl's family's house in Maine, this seemed somehow inevitable, but in the abject poverty of Appalachia, our wedding plans feel both extravagant and unforgivable. The abundance of choice we have in deciding something as simple as hors d'oeuvres feels utterly foreign as we pass decaying barns, shacks held together by rusted corrugated metal, dirt yards with scrawny, mud-caked livestock resting lethargically by ragged fencing.

Goats have long been a presence in the granite mountains of Tennessee; their incredible versatility has made them indispensable. In some parts of the state groups are actively showing purebred goats, but in eastern Tennessee the animals are respected for their utility more than their grace. There the image of scrub goats providing milk and meat to families in need is fresher and stronger than that of registered does and sanctioned shows. Goats are a hillbilly sort of animal: useful, hard scrabblers, masters at getting by. In them, in a comical, self-deprecating sort of way, people see a little bit of themselves. The term *hillbilly*, though it comes from another etymological source, conjures their form.

While researching meat goats, we came across a goat association that prizes animals for exactly these qualities, emphatically rejecting the notion of goats as show animals. Not surprisingly, the organization's heart is in eastern Tennessee.

Camping in a nearby state park, we drive to Jamestown, Tennessee, in search of the Mountain Goat Ranch, a Kiko goat farm owned by Ruble Conatser, president of the American Kiko Goat Association. *Kiko* is the Maori word for meat or flesh, and the Kiko goat, we've learned through some preliminary research, was developed by ranchers in New Zealand in the mid-1980s. At the time feral goats roamed the Kiwi wilderness, descendants of animals brought to New Zealand by eighteenth-century European settlers. Modern ranchers rounded up females from the wild herds and bred them to domesticated bucks. The results were a new generation of goats with the size of their meat-goat fathers and the strength and natural parasite resistance that hundreds of years of natural selection had given their mothers. By 1986, the breed name Kiko was established; in the early 1990s, when Boer goats were first introduced to America, Kikos also began to make their way to the United States.

As we creep up the steep drive, we see the Kikos for the first time. Wandering the open pasture on land dotted with craggy rocks and patches of brush, the animals are impressive: wide, scimitar horns; shaggy white coats; massive, powerful bodies. Ruble isn't home yet when we arrive, so we spend a few minutes just watching the goats. They look almost wild, more like mythic creatures than domestic animals.

When Ruble arrives, we meet a strong, fit man in an ironed shirt tucked into snug jeans, a big belt buckle, and cowboy boots. Except for his wire-rimmed glasses, he looks every inch the farmer. Stopping inside just long enough to say hello to his wife, he leads us to the back pastures to look more closely at the animals while we talk. His Anatolian shepherds—guard dogs who look incredibly like Godfrey, though three times his size—eye us warily.

Ruble is a social worker by day, a detail that completely surprises us. Somehow we have in mind, maybe from our experience with Dave Bernier, that meat goat farmers are necessarily tough guys. Ruble's got the pickup truck and the belt buckle, but in his professional life he helps others get back on track, and that complexity of his character reminds us why we love the goat world.

His background also helps him frame his argument for goats; understanding firsthand how an initial prejudice can sabotage the best intentions, he also sees the flip side, how exploiting that prejudice can work to one's advantage. When it comes to goats, Ruble's plan is all in the marketing. After more than a decade in the meat goat world, he's firmly convinced that goat is the meat of the future. It's lean and tasty, and especially in the South, the animal uses resources efficiently, feeding itself while clearing out kudzu, amusing itself on the uneven terrain.

The trouble is the stigma, but Ruble intends to turn that on its head. Capitalizing on the goat's hillbilly connotations, he's making Horny Goat Jerky, dried patties of highly spiced ground meat that he plans to market throughout the South and eventually the country. The jerky is currently in development, and piling into his pickup, Ruble takes us down the road to show us his production facility. Still in the early stages, at this point it's simply a squat cinder-block building with cavernous rooms and a large freezer of goat meat. For Ruble, however, it's all mapped out.

"This is my office, this is the production line, this is storage," he gestures as we tour each empty white room. With his enthusiasm, we can see it too.

Eventually, Ruble would like to sell fresh goat meat and jerky. Opening a large chest freezer, he shows us his branding of the fresh meat. Sold in the three most popular cuts of beef (steaks, ground, and in patties), each package is marked with a patriotic "Made in Tennessee" label and the USDA Grade A certification seal. The meat never comes from bucks ("too goaty"), and in its packaging, looks just like beef. It's all part of the plan, and Ruble is confident that the meat will take off. "It's just a matter of time."

Later that evening in his living room, Ruble offers us samples from some early batches of jerky. He pulls out hand-labeled Ziploc bags, each holding a few flat, brown disks. Jerky is simply dried, spiced meat. Though in this country it's generally made from beef, it can be made from any meat; in South Africa, Karl and I tried some made from kudu and springbok. Ruble's jerky is made from ground meat, so its texture is rough and a little pebbled. Rather than pulling off in strings, following the grain of the muscle, the goat jerky breaks off into pieces when bitten. It's chewy, not at all goaty, and though the spices are top secret, there's an underlying sweetness that makes me suspect molasses. We ask if we can buy some for the road, but Ruble just laughs and hands us a couple of bags.

As dusk falls, Ruble invites us to stay for supper with his family. The Conatsers don't have children of their own, but they are raising Ruble's teenage niece, who peppers us with questions about life in New York. As we tell her about life in the city, she keeps shaking her head and asking, "Why did you leave?" Though we try to explain, she refuses to believe that it was because we wanted a life more like hers.

Dinner itself is chicken-fried goat with mashed potatoes and gravy. We've come to consider ourselves connoisseurs of goat meat, but had Ruble not told us that we were eating goat, we would never have known. Fried in a crisp golden batter, covered in rich gravy, the meat is a little peppery, but hasn't a hint of gaminess. We know that he invited us out of generosity and a sense of southern hospitality, but Ruble has also proven his point.

Leaving the ranch after dark, we drive by pastures of ghostly white creatures barely illuminated in a great bowl of stars. In addition to the packages of jerky, Ruble has given us a cooler full of frozen goat patties and steaks. He's also slapped a bumper sticker on our car: Eat More Goat.

Chapter 7

W

e spend a few days camping in the Great Smoky Mountains, using Ruble's meat to make improvised goat chili over the fire for dinner. (Fry ground meat in skillet, add one can of spiced beans: dinner.) Continuing south, we make our way to Split Creek Farm, just minutes outside the trim town center of Anderson, South Carolina.

Down a winding red dirt lane, amid palmettos, pines, and live oaks, we find a farm that is completely in harmony with its setting. Low-slung old buildings with wide wooden porches have been rehabbed to accommodate farm offices, and open pastures stretch out into woods that ring the property. Crawling up the long drive, we are greeted by a succession of animals that include a wandering flock of chickens, a pair of potbellied pigs named Caroline and Reggie, a hutch of rabbits, and, resting comfortably on top of a picnic table, a sweet beige Toggenburg doe. After we nose around the barn and outbuildings and various pens of goats for a few minutes, the human proprietors of the farm, Evin Evans and Pat Bell, spot us and call out hello.

We had met Evin and Pat at the ADGA convention where we attended a marketing workshop Evin gave. Calling on members to unite and work harder in their promotion of the goat, Evin had impressed us with her homey style. Harsh truths came from her in a sweet southern accent that made them impossible to dispute or resent. ("Invest in marketing, folks," she told the crowd, "Think about branding. Find a logo and plaster it all over everything you can—T-shirts, stickers, your truck." Her words resonated, as we were doing much the same thing to fund our project. I passed a note to Karl—"Should we make stickers?")

Pat, a nationally renowned folk artist, had donated several painted goat silhouettes to a fund-raising auction at the convention, and some of her smaller works had been for sale, along with Split Creek's fromage blanc and award-winning oil-cured feta at the Split Creek booth in the vendor area. Evin, with short salt-and-pepper hair, a raspy voice, and an easy smile, came and went, attending to business as an active ADGA member and dairy goat judge. Pat, a gentle, motherly figure, stayed put, patiently answering questions about her work and their cheese. We hung around the booth like shy teenagers, fishing for an invitation to the farm. Eventually, our persistence paid off.

When we'd asked Evin at the ADGA convention how she got into goats, she'd taken no time to reply, "It's pretty simple because goats got into me. There's no question about it that when I was a child I knew that I was a goat person."

She explained further that thirty years ago, when she was partway through her studies in animal science at Clemson University, she was told that it was impossible for her to become a goat farmer. It was understood in the department that however much she might study, to become a farmer Evin would need "to marry it or bury it. Farming on my own just wasn't presented as an option."

A wiry, energetic woman, who is also openly gay, Evin went on to be the first female graduate in the animal science department and then to defy convention by starting a dairy goat operation. Since then, she has become widely respected for the quality of her animals, her feed program, and her herd management. She has also become a passionate advocate for women in agriculture, and to that end, all of the farm's full-time employees are female. In our travels, this is the first farm we've come to that is entirely self-supporting; while it may not turn a huge profit, Split Creek Farm funds itself.

Split Creek Farm is a Grade A commercial dairy, the first of its kind that we visit. The distinction of being a Grade A dairy is a huge one, and something we were totally ignorant of until our immersion in the dairy goat world at the ADGA convention. In contrast to uncertified farms or Grade B dairies, which cannot legally sell fluid milk for human consumption, Grade A dairies can bottle their milk, sell it through distributors, and market their products across state lines. Though each state has its own dairy regulations, the stringent sanitation guidelines of Grade A dairies are respected throughout the United States. All milk bought in grocery stores, for instance, has come from a Grade A dairy, and most of it has crossed state lines. While it is more costly for a farm to adhere to these regulations, it can be worth its while, especially for cheese makers working in Grade A dairies who can export their products across the country.

Unlike most states, South Carolina is one of a handful to allow Grade A dairies to legally sell raw milk. Raw milk, the common name for milk that has not been pasteurized, is the subject of much debate in the United States. For its advocates, among them Max Mc-Calman, it represents a more natural, less-processed approach to dairy products. It is strained to eliminate foreign materials, but raw milk is not heat-treated, nor is it generally homogenized. Beneath a thick layer of cream, the milk is straight from the udder, rich with flavorful fats and beneficial enzymes and bacteria.

It is these elements, however, that cause controversy. Raw milk's detractors claim that hiding in the milk may be other harmful pathogens, such as the bacterium *Listeria monocytogenes*, *Staphylococcus aureus*, or the bacillus E. coli, any of which can be deadly. Advocates of raw milk counter that these pathogens have become more problematic in recent decades because humans no longer have the immunity to them that was once built up over a lifetime of mild exposure. Raw milk, they assert, works as a kind of inoculation against these bacteria.

Pasteurization kills all pathogens and also lengthens the shelf life of milk. Because of its active bacteria and microflora, raw milk spoils much more quickly than pasteurized. Organizations such as the Weston A. Price Foundation and the Right to Choose Healthy Food campaign cast a skeptical eye on dairy legislation, arguing that regulations are created largely in favor of big business. If small farms cannot legally sell raw milk in their communities, the only milk available is that which can be found in the dairy cases at the grocery store. Laws that restrict raw-milk sales, advocates claim, are therefore actively contributing to the decline of small farming while also keeping consumers from access to products they desire to the point of criminalizing their pursuit.

Across America, people have tried to circumvent these laws. Since it's legal to drink raw milk from one's own animals, a farmer in Wisconsin sold shares of his dairy cows, then bottled the milk for their "owners." In New York City, a "raw-milk coven" in Hell's Kitchen imported unpasteurized milk from Amish dairy farmers in Pennsylvania. On farm porches around the country, surreptitious raw-milk sales are conducted by "donation": patrons bring their own bottles and leave whatever money they think is fair in a cash box.

South Carolina's milk legislation is a rarity in this world of raw dairy on the sly. Seen as either progressive or antiquated, the state's regulations allow Grade A dairies to sell their fluid milk raw, though they are restricted to selling it within the state. Because of this, Split Creek has developed two very distinct markets for its products. Locally, it sells fresh, unpasteurized goat's milk at the farm shop and at farmers' markets, while nationally the farm is known for its award-winning cheeses made with pasteurized milk and available in stores, at restaurants throughout the Southeast, and by mail.

Unlike many cheese makers who use raw milk specifically for the complexity it brings to their aged cheeses, Evin prefers to make an assortment of fresh cheeses and some cured fetas, all of which she makes with pasteurized milk. She does so in part because it's easier to market on a large scale, and in part because it keeps her cheeses out of the politics of raw milk. The cheeses are clearly not suffering from pasteurization; two years after our visit, in a cheese competition judged by Max McCalman, Split Creek's pasteurized Feta Marinated in Oil takes home Best in Show.

Camping at night on the red-clay shores of the lake at a nearby state park, our visit to the farm spans two days. Upon our arrival, Evin invites us to join a tour of the farm that she's about to lead for a dairy goat club from the Outer Banks. The members of the club are predominantly hobby farmers, retirees who have discovered goats late in their lives and are learning as they go. Among them we meet a former engineer at NBC who has found the joys of the country after a lifetime in Manhattan. They've all arranged for goat-sitters and joke about their busman's holiday, checking in on their own animals by cell phone as they visit other farms throughout the state.

As a group, we explore the barns and the pastures, observing Evin's strict biohazard policies (before entering anywhere the animals can go, we must dip our shoes in a disinfectant bath). While distractedly scratching a young doe, I look down to find that she's chewed through the cord of our microphone.

At the end of the tour, Pat invites the group into the farm store, where she's arranged samples of products made with Split Creek's milk. In addition to plain and herbed fresh logs of chèvre, their cheeses include savory and sweet varieties of goat fromage blanc, cheese balls rolled in almonds and local pecans, and their famous cubed fetas soaked in brine, wrapped dry, and marinated in olive oil with herbs and sun-dried tomatoes. We try a little of everything, admiring the clean tang of plain chèvre, lingering over the fresh sweetness and delicate texture of peach fromage blanc. The firm bites of marinated feta are extraordinary, crumbling against our teeth, absorbing a piney hint of rosemary and marrying it with the pungency of the cheese.

To accompany squares of rich goat's milk fudge—cubes of deep chocolate, dotted generously with pecans—we're handed Dixie cups of raw goat's milk. Surprisingly to us, several of the goat owners are reluctant to drink the milk; apparently, they raise their animals solely to show.

Thick, sweet, and creamy, the milk tastes nothing like the ultra-pasteurized goat's milk we've bought in the grocery store. Its flavor is not excessively goaty, but it is earthier, more mammalian. On our palates, it is clear that what we're tasting is close to the source. In this one paper cup, we're reminded of our motivations in embarking on this great goat journey. Incredibly, it is something as sweet and simple, as primal as milk that keeps us focused on our ultimate goals.

The next morning, we wake to the reflection of water on our tent roof. Arriving early at the farm we're greeted by Evin and Maggie Miller, a Clemson graduate who works as the assistant farm manager. They offer us steaming cups of strong coffee, Evin advising, "there's nothing like a little goat's milk in your coffee." I pour in a splash from a pitcher in the kitchen and discover that she's right.

This is our first commercial milking, and we have no idea what to expect. Split Creek's herd, which is predominantly made up of Nubian goats, comprises several hundred animals, about half of which are lactating at any one time. As we walk toward the milking parlor, Evin explains that the goats are milked twice a day and because of the sheer number of animals, they are milked by machine. The machine works with a system of vacuum pumps that suck the milk from the animal's teats, then sends it through a suspended maze of glass tubing and a filtration system, and finally deposits it in a cooling tank. From there, the milk is either bottled raw or it's pasteurized and made into cheese.

We have only seen animals being milked into buckets by hand, never by machine, and certainly not by a system as intricate as this. We watch in fascination as the apparatus comes to life, with foamy white milk shooting through its transparent tubes, but we're also astonished to see how much human contact is still involved in the milking. When the does are led onto the milking platform, their udders are still "stripped" by hand, meaning that the first squirt of milk is squeezed by someone's fingers rather than the pump. The suction pumps are attached and removed manually, and when they are finished, the teats are all sterilized by hand.

Over the roaring noise of the pump, Evin and Maggie talk to the goats while scratching their ears and shoulders. Each doe has her own habits and personality, and the women know them all, their rhythms and their tricks. Though we were expecting the machine to take all of the intimacy out of milking, it actually still feels like a very personal time with the goats. Maybe it's the hour or the breaking light, but in spite of the noise and the bustle and all of the work, milking seems to us an ideal way to begin the morning. This meditative closeness to the animals, even in the midst of clamoring machines and tight schedules, is a direction in which we can imagine ourselves going.

Before leaving, we ask Evin what she loves about her goats. She replies with no hesitation, "That they are truly partners on the farm. We're obviously connected on some other level."

We feel inklings of that, too—not in any kind of strange metaphysical sense, but in a pragmatic way, grounded in the actions we will need to take to realize that connection. Bouncing down the drive of Split Creek Farm, half a dozen jars of marinating feta nestled among our camping gear, we feel the inevitability of an agricultural existence and a renewed longing for the life we hope to create.

Chapter 8

We spend Thanksgiving in Florida where my father has flown out to meet Karl's parents. (Golf is played; all is well.) At dinner, we're joined by an impeccably dressed elderly Canadian widow who's moved south in retirement. We tell her about our project, and she, like so many others, counters with a goat story of her own.

"My father owned an abattoir in Toronto," she begins, "and when I was a child there was one goat who was virtually an employee. I can't remember his name. His job was to lead the other animals into the chute—I know it's horrible—and the men who worked for my father loved him. They'd take him out drinking at night, and give him cigarette butts to chew on. When he died, they shut down the plant for the day because everyone was in mourning." She looks wistful for a moment, then smiles, "That must sound crazy." Actually, we tell her, not at all.

While in Florida, we finalize our wedding guest list and send out save-the-date cards, choosing an illustration that Karl's found on the

Internet. It's a woodcut of a goat standing upright, propped on a walking stick, and draped in a cloak. We think it's a perfect blend of travel, tradition, and goats. It's not until my mother receives hers and calls us, horrified, that we learn that in medieval iconography this image represented the devil.

Back on the road, we find ourselves in an unseasonably (unreasonably) cold winter. Camping in Florida's exemplary system of state parks—where armadillos trundle into the spiny underbrush and makeshift neighborhoods of RV dwellers encourage us to use their communal citrus juicers—the nights sometimes dip into the high twenties, and we wake to find the tent frosty and the dog huddled between our sleeping bags. In the afternoons, the temperatures rise comfortably, but by sunset—which comes earlier every day—we are chilled, holding our evening debate over comfort and frugality.

"Wouldn't a motel be a nice treat?" I suggest, knowing that the more we stay in motels, the less of a treat they become.

"How much money do we have?" Karl inevitably counters, usually with one raised eyebrow. Thrift generally wins.

We're on our way to Kevuda Haven, a farm that we hope will give us some insight into the demand for *cabrito*—goat meat—in Miami's extensive Latino community. After crossing Alligator Alley and weaving our way up Florida's western coast, we take a slight detour inland. I cannot think of a less hospitable place to raise animals than south-central Florida. The natural predators are vast and varied. From above are hawks and turkey vultures, from below are coral snakes and rattlesnakes, and just creeping along the earth are alligators, coyotes, black widows, and brown recluse spiders with which to contend. Six months of the year the climate is unbearably hot and humid, brambles grow thick and spread quickly; where land is cleared, rain often turns it to swamp.

As we drive through the back roads lined with moss-draped trees and billboards that read things like "Do you have a chronic wound that won't heal? Call The Wound Center," we don't expect to see viable farmland, much less an organized Boer goat ranch. The brackish canals on either side of the county road to Kevuda Haven seem unlikely to give way to dry land, and certainly not to the kinds of open pastures necessary to maintain meat goats. Yet there, past the sign and a mezuzah, it lies.

The word *Kevuda* means "precious" in Hebrew, and Larry Krech, a former grocer and the owner of Kevuda Haven, has worked hard to make his land worthy of the name. When he bought the property twelve years ago, it was thickly forested and waist-deep in blackberry cane. He began to clear the land, and during the process someone suggested to him that a few goats might help to keep the brush at bay. He fell in love with the animals, and the farm has grown out of that affection.

When we pull in front of his house, Larry comes out to meet us. He has thick, silvery-white hair and a full beard, and looks a bit like Kenny Rogers. Shuffling a little, he apologizes in advance that he might be moving a little slowly because prostate cancer that had been in remission has come back. "I've just finished a round of radiation therapy," he says, and Karl and I immediately apologize for intruding on his recuperation. He waves it off.

Still an impressive presence in a denim shirt and black cowboy hat, Larry tells us that for the last year, as he's been focusing on his health, he's turned over much of the herd management for his three hundred goats to Ronald Cordero, a young Venezuelan man he'll introduce us to, who lives with his wife and baby in one of the outbuildings. Though Ronald was a graphic designer in Venezuela, he's quickly getting a feel for goats. Following Larry—whose step quickens as he nears the goats—we find Ronald methodically trimming hooves in the buck pasture.

Ronald is a relatively inexperienced goatherd, but Larry trusts him implicitly with the care of his animals. One reason for this is that the men share a religious faith and actually became acquainted through their Messianic Jewish congregation, Beit Yisrael. The men and their families keep kosher, post mezuzot on their doorframes, observe the Sabbath on Saturday, pray in Hebrew, and celebrate the Jewish holidays as prescribed in Leviticus, such as Passover and Sukkot. Yet they also believe that Christ is the Messiah.

As Larry shows us his farm and we speak about the land and his religious beliefs—he's delighted to learn that we're Jewish—he and Ronald continue to perform the day's work. Trailing behind, we ask about the market for goat meat in Miami.

"Well, we do sell some animals for meat to customers who visit the ranch, but really the fun is in the breeding. We're trying to raise the best meat goats possible, not necessarily for show, but for the hardiest genetics and the meatiest frame."

He has a strictly regulated breeding program to produce animals that will conform to his standards; during our visit, several does are due to kid and he's looking forward to seeing the results. While Ronald gets feed ready for most of the animals, Larry goes into the pasture to check on one goat that has isolated herself from the hungry herd. We're waiting by the fence when Larry begins waving his arms and shouting for us to come into the pasture.

"Hurry, hurry!" he calls. Gathering our cameras and notepads, we rush into the field.

There, one kid is lying on the ground under its mother, while another is poking out of her, its hooves and head hanging below her tail. The goat looks exhausted and uncomfortable, and at intervals she makes low bleating sounds. She seems to be steeling herself, then with one final push, the kid slides out in a gush of afterbirth, and immediately the mother, a red Spanish doe with one curled horn, begins to lick her baby and nibble the sandy placenta from its head.

Gradually she cleans them up, and the two Boer-cross kids—one black and white, the other red and white—begin to wobble and squawk, tumbling over each other and craning their necks to find their mama's teats.

Karl and I have never been present at a birth. We stand there watching, our mouths open, tears forming in the corners of our eyes. It is overwhelming, truly a miracle that these little animals come out, their translucent hooves and downy fur perfect from the very beginning. In the same pasture, two kids that have been born earlier in the morning are snuggled in some tall grass while their mother stands a way off, expelling the last bloody strings of afterbirth. Larry explains that some mothers immediately take to their kids, cleaning and hovering protectively over them, while others are distracted by feed or shade. Last year, he said, one of his does had rolled over onto her babies, smothering them. Most, though, he assures us, are good mothers, "Just like humans."

We're on the high of new life when we leave Kevuda Haven. We can't stop talking about the baby goats.

"Can you believe it? I mean, it was so fast, it just came shooting out!" I babble on, excitedly. What we've seen is unbelievable: a little goat entering the world, taking its first breaths, making its first sounds, its world completely new. It seems impossible that we have watched the beginning of another creature's life. We feel as though the day has been charmed by these sweet, small animals.

After a few hours of driving, we pull into a state park on the outskirts of Leesburg, Florida, making it past the ranger's booth just before the gates close for the evening. We settle into our campsite, then go in search of the bathrooms. As we approach them, we're disconcerted to see the back of a small body hunched in a corner beneath an oversized, black down parka. On public radio, we've just heard a story about burgeoning crime in state and national parks—specifically, about the production and distribution of crystal meth—

and I immediately whisper to Karl that I think we've stumbled into a drug ring.

When the parka turns around, however, I feel ridiculous to find a little old man doing his laundry. His name is Charlie Hancock, and while Karl and I take turns alternately brushing our teeth and holding Godfrey, we strike up a conversation. Charlie is from the Midwest and is on his way to visit his daughter for the holidays. He asks us where we're from and, though it's not completely true, we tell him Maine.

"When I was in the service, I knew a Kip Fletcher from Maine," Charlie says, "But I haven't seen him in almost fifty years." Then he catches himself, chuckling. What are the odds that we would know his Air Force buddy?

Actually, very good. As it turns out, Cliff Fletcher, "Kip" in his youth, was Karl's father's business partner for thirty years. On our cell phone, we call Cliff, then hand the phone over to Charlie. Twenty minutes later, he finds us at our campsite, tears in his eyes. The two men hadn't spoken since Cliff threw Charlie a going-away party in Japan in the late 1950s. For all of us, the day is like magic. Falling asleep in our tent, we wonder aloud why we said we were from Maine? It would have been so much closer to the truth to say we were from New York, but for some reason it just doesn't seem right anymore.

In the morning, we take some pictures of Charlie in front of his Winnebago to send to Cliff, then continue on our way to Auburn, Alabama, where we're headed to the epicenter of research on goat reproduction: the College of Veterinary Medicine at Auburn University.

Auburn's teaching hospital is airy and orderly. It is known especially for its work with large-animal reproduction—notably, surgeries to correct penile dysfunctions in bulls—and animals are brought from as far away as Texas for semen collection, analysis, and sometimes surgery. Racehorses, champion bulls, and, especially in the last few years, Boer goats find their way to Auburn for a variety of procedures that examine and, when necessary, enhance their fertility. As the Boer industry has grown, and semen from champion bucks has become prized, research in goat reproduction has kept pace. While bulls are still Auburn's specialty, its goat program is by all accounts superb, largely due to the efforts of David Pugh, editor of the textbook *Sheep and Goat Medicine*, and one of the country's leading researchers in the field of small ruminant reproduction.

We've come to Auburn to talk goats with Dr. Pugh and his colleague Leslie Lawhorn, a veterinarian and researcher who is also working on goat reproduction. When we arrive, Dr. Pugh has been unexpectedly called to a meeting, and Dr. Lawhorn is paged for us at the reception desk. A woman about our age, Dr. Lawhorn isn't immediately recognizable as a veterinarian. With her loose brown hair and well-cut clothing, she seems more like a movie star playing the part. Fresh from performing a goat sonogram, she offers us a tour of the hospital.

The building has the same feel as a human hospital, but since the animals who come there are so massive, the rooms are built on a much larger and easier-to-clean scale. The ceilings are high, the doors are wide and latch securely, and the concrete floors slope gently to a drain. It doesn't smell of animals, there are no bits of hay or dung to mark lingering traces of their presence, but it doesn't have the same sterile feel as a hospital. Karl and I marvel at all of it—it's so different, so much better funded, than any other veterinary office we've seen.

Dr. Lawhorn leads us through the progression of rooms an animal would be taken to if brought in for treatment, explaining the process as we go. We begin outside, where there are barns for boarding and a "lameness assessment arena," where the animals are first examined. Inside are more examining rooms, with stanchions to keep the animals still during more thorough and, for those with reproductive issues, more personal inspections. If surgery is warranted, they are then led to a padded room, where anesthesia is administered. Once the animal is tranquilized, it's hooked to a harness in a track in the ceiling that suspends the body and swings it to the operating room where there are lights and equipment much as there would be in a human operating room, but no bed for the patient to lie on. Surgery is conducted with the animal in a standing position, supported from the ceiling by a sling. Following a procedure, the animal is moved to an indoor stall for recovery. If a foal or calf is involved, it's usually placed on a gurney rimmed with padded bumpers—much like a vastly oversized crib—until it's well enough to stand in a stall. At a central station, doctors and students keep a constant monitor on the patient's recovery. As the three of us walk by, a group of them are eating lunch while keeping an eye on a cluster of black and white monitors.

Though most of the veterinarians have offices on the second floor of the hospital, the goat research facility is located in another building a short distance away. Following Dr. Lawhorn's Land Rover in our Goat Mobile, we drive to their offices—on our way passing a very tall man loping along, leading his camel on a rope—then on through cow pastures to a small building and a set of barns.

"A lot of our aspiring veterinarians have never spent time on a farm," Dr. Lawhorn explains, "so at Auburn we introduce them to the daily care of livestock, as well as medical treatments." New students are required to take part in caring for the college's herd of cattle, performing farm chores as part of their education.

Inside the research facility, Dr. Lawhorn shows us her laboratory, which is filled with microscopes, glass tubes, and various machines that look complicated and, to our eyes, very scientific. She also shows us her equipment for semen collection: an artificial vagina and an electric ejaculator.

Not being scientists, it's easy for us to forget that analysis always begins with the clean collection of a sample. In the case of goat reproduction, that means gathering semen. In all the talk we've heard about artificial insemination and "buck collection," I haven't really considered what it entails. Looking at the rubber sheath and the sort of rounded-off rocket, I understand a little better why farmers often hire professionals to collect their bucks.

As we're poking around the lab, Dr. Pugh comes in to introduce himself. A stocky, voluble, bald man in a wrestling sweatshirt (he coaches at a local high school), he speaks quickly and in a thick southern accent, suggesting that we all go to the barns to look at the goats. "My day is *crazy*," he says emphatically. He's due back at another meeting, so we talk along the way.

The son of a west Georgia farmer who once kept a herd of his own goats, Dr. Pugh has watched the changing tides of goat keeping in the region and has strong opinions about farming and animal management. Though he instructs students and owners on preventative measures, he believes that the ideal scenario would be one in which animals have been bred for natural resistance to parasites and disease, much like the Kikos we visited in Tennessee. If a serious illness, like caprine encephalitis or scrapies, occurs in a herd, Dr. Pugh says, pointing his finger at us to underscore his point, "I believe in a scorched-earth policy. I'm serious, my favorite textbook for disease management is Machiavelli's *The Prince*." He grins.

Because he is such a charismatic person and because he backs everything up with science, Dr. Pugh can say things like this without sounding crazy. His enthusiasm for the animals, too, is contagious, and it seems entirely likely that support for Auburn's goat program has grown through the sheer force of Dr. Pugh's energy. Though he'll work on other livestock, he tells us, "My favorite animal is the meat goat. Absolutely."

In the barn, we can see in his interaction with the Boers how much genuine affection he has for the animals. While we're there, Dr. Pugh asks if we'd like to see a sonogram; he's scheduled to perform one on a Boer doe. The four of us enter the stall and while Dr. Lawhorn holds the goat, Dr. Pugh gently runs a wand over her belly. Like a human sonogram, the image appears on a monitor in fuzzy, moving, black and white. Pointing to the screen, Dr. Pugh distinguishes for our untrained eyes which little blobs are goats ("Naw, that's just amniotic fluid over there."). He presses a button on the machine and hands us a picture of two tiny goat fetuses.

This is what all the research is about; the semen collection, the penile surgery, the embryo transfers are simply a means to this end. As he points to the screen, Dr. Pugh smiles and says, "Look, there's an angel, and there's an angel."

To see animals that will make it to the meat market—instead of the rarified goats that come through the veterinary hospital—Dr. Pugh recommends that we visit the Saturday goat auction at the Circle H Auction House in Brundidge, Alabama. A weekly event for decades, the auction in Brundidge is held at a house that auctions off everything from random household items to poultry to (on the day that we visit) a pair of miniature donkeys.

We spend the night in a local state park. Sandwiched between two prisons, it is cold and desolate, the sky illuminated on both sides by the glow of security lights. We try to cheer ourselves by watching episodes of *The Simpsons* on our laptop, but we sleep fitfully in the front seat of the car, cocooned upright in our sleeping bags, turning the engine on every few hours to blast warm air. Before dawn, we awaken cold and stiff and leave for the auction.

Approaching the town of Brundidge, we pass through a series of classic southern hamlets. A bright mural on the side of a warehouse marks the beginning of one block of downtown storefronts that peters quickly back to a rural route. In another, a water tower advertises that we've reached the home of an annual Peanut Butter Festival and birthplace of baseball player Don Sutton. At one time the area clearly boasted civic pride, but now Brundidge, with a population of roughly two thousand, whose median household income is less than $17,000 a year, is, by the gray early light, bleak. Searching for a local diner for breakfast, we find only a Hardee's on the edge of the highway.

At the auction house, we discover that the morning is devoted to the miscellany (read: attic junk) sale, then followed by the poultry auction. The goats won't be auctioned until after one. While waiting for the goat sale to begin, we chat with the locals. Jerry Smith, the former owner of the Circle H Auction House, tells us he's had goats since he was twelve, but in the last fifteen years, Alabama's meat goat business has noticeably grown.

Leaning against a picnic table, a man called Jumper seconds that. With a broad belly and long black beard, Jumper has the look of a pirate. He tells us that he's been selling goats to buyers in Miami for the past forty years, but that the largest goat auctions are the ones that supply the New York area.

"The New Holland, Pennsylvania, auctions," he says, "That's where the real money is."

Talking intermittently on his cell phone, Jumper explains to us how he brings goats to the Miami market. After buying the animals from various auction houses, he takes them to his farm for a month or two to fatten up, then hauls them down to Florida. He's a little cagey about the location of his farm and also about his clients; it occurs to us that perhaps the live meat markets he sells to are not entirely legal. Worse, we've just read an article about the slaughter of live goats in Santeria and Voodoo rituals, and though Jumper says nothing explicit, the idea that this might make up some of his sales lingers. When his phone rings again, we politely wander off.

As much as anything else, we get the feeling that the Saturday morning auctions are Brundidge's main social event. Half the town must be there, buying hot dogs and beans from the concession, commenting on the animals in pens behind the house.

Though the clientele is a little different, the auction itself is not unlike the one we attended in Maine. Thin goats are led individually into a stuffy, smoky arena, where for the most part, three main livestock dealers bid on them. There are a few families there looking for Christmas pets, but the majority of bidders, like Jumper, will be re-selling the animals for meat. The goats look underfed and a little gooey around the nose, and it amazes me that dealers will pay anything for them, then it makes me sad that they bid so little. After seeing the twin miracles of goats in the womb and the wonder of birth, the auction where those little lives could end up simply makes me feel low. Outside a light drizzle has turned to cold rain, and after about an hour we can't take much more. We decide to get back on the road, anxious to leave the morning behind.

Chapter 9

Crossing through Mississippi and into Louisiana, we feel a lightening of spirits, brought on more by our proximity to the Gulf Coast than by any change in our situation. The nights are still frigid and we are still facing the daily calculus between tent and motel, but pre-Katrina, the landscape is wonderful. In Biloxi, pillared mansions are set back behind gates, their driveways lined by trees tinseled with Spanish moss. At Mississippi's Buccaneer State Park, we walk Godfrey on the beach and try to make out whether a wooden shaft poking out of the water is the mast of a sunken ship. On the outskirts of New Orleans, we sample oyster po'boys and learn to suck the brains out of a pile of spicy boiled crawfish. In Baton Rouge, we explore preserved plantations and eat gumbo in a converted slave shack.

Far inland, tucked in the laces of Louisiana's boot, we meet Chef John Folse, self-described Cajun ambassador to the world, and Cindi McDonald, goatherd, at the farm that houses their joint dairy goat venture in Jackson, Louisiana. Though Cindi has kept goats on and off for more than twenty years, Chef Folse's association with the animals at first seems unlikely. A restaurateur with his own line of packaged Cajun foods, Chef Folse (everyone calls him that) is the host of a public television show, opened a Cajun restaurant in Moscow, and, we learn in the course of our conversation, once cooked a private meal for Pope John Paul II. His Lafitte's Landing Restaurant in Donaldsonville and his White Oak Plantation in Baton Rouge are acclaimed for their renditions of regional classics; the Chef John Folse Culinary Institute at Nicholls State University honors his passion for the preservation of Louisiana's culinary heritage.

A prolific cookbook author, Chef Folse discovered the recipe for an almost extinct Creole cream cheese while researching his seventh book, *The Encyclopedia of Cajun and Creole Cuisine*. The cheese is a soft, fresh, acid-set, single curd brought to the area by the French in the eighteenth or nineteenth century. Traditionally made at home or in the area's small commercial dairies, Creole cream cheese is a classic farmer's cheese, made with a combination of skim milk and buttermilk. In old recipes, it's often served with fruit preserves and a splash of cream. In his research, Chef Folse found that the cheese had been a staple of the Creole diet until state regulations made it difficult for dairies selling fluid milk to also make cheese in the same facility. As dairies consolidated and focused on producing one or the other, the native cream cheese began to die out, and by the mid-1980s it was virtually gone. Chef Folse decided to resurrect it.

Adding Bittersweet Plantation Dairy to his collection of culinary enterprises, Chef Folse began to experiment with cow's milk and goat's milk cheeses, and to search for partners. In Cindi McDonald, he found an experienced goatherd, who, after some years without animals, was ready to start farming again. In the world of goat dairies, this kind of partnership is rare—as the buyer, Chef Folse has a say in the type of milk he's after, as the seller, Cindi McDonald has a guaranteed market. As the two tell us almost in chorus, it's a win-win situation.

McDonald's farm is nestled among pecan and pine trees off a small country road. When we arrive, we find a flurry of activity and, in Cindi McDonald, an unlikely goatherd. Dressed in a pantsuit under a long, fur-collared coat, McDonald's hair is smooth and coiffed and her face is tastefully made up. The morning is bright but chilly, and she offers us coffee from a thermos while we await the arrival of Chef Folse, who is coming from his office. Except for the long wooden crook she keeps in her car and her clear knowledge of and affection for her animals, we would never have guessed her occupation; in appearance and aspect, she seems more realtor than farmer.

After a few minutes, Chef Folse and his director of communications, Michaela York, come rambling up the drive in a sleek black SUV. From the choice of car, we're expecting someone in a suit and tie, more comfortable in the city than the country. But stepping out of the driver's seat, dressed in a plaid flannel shirt and jeans, Chef Folse seems utterly at home on the farm, and delighted to be there. "I don't come out here that often," he explains, and he fairly bounces over to see the progress of the milking parlor, "but every time I come I say 'Wow! That's new since I was here last!'"

Inside a flat cinder-block rectangle, workers are assembling milk stands that will eventually accommodate twenty goats at a time. McDonald hopes to expand her herd to two hundred milking does, and though Chef Folse's goat cheeses are still in development, he's confident that he'll be able to use all the milk she can produce. His philosophy, he explains to us, is to approach his calculations from a success quotient. "I go in saying, if we do it, we're going to be successful at it," he says, "so what's the biggest milk vat I can get?"

People, especially those who work in Chef Folse's manufacturing plant, often consider his strategy strange and a little imprudent, but his boundless energy and optimism is born out of a combination of faith in his instinct and a willingness to do whatever it takes to succeed. An example of this from McDonald's farm: Chef Folse regularly sends out the carpenters, refrigeration specialists, and electricians he has on staff at his New Orleans production facility to help speed the work along. Though he admits that some of these workers—especially one who happened to arrive when the goats had gotten loose—think that the enterprise is nuts, he's eager to move things along as quickly as possible, so he's not asking McDonald to reimburse him yet. "Eventually," he says, "we'll just trade out that work in milk."

At Bittersweet Plantation Dairy, Chef Folse's full-steam-ahead method has also been bolstered by the validation he's received for the cheeses he already has in production. Mother Noella Marcellino, the Connecticut nun who has gained world renown as a cheese maker, scientist, and raw-milk advocate, has judged his cow milk cheeses to be exceptional, and in the process has become a friend.

"When I brought my cheese to her . . . you can imagine just the fear of that because here I am, I don't know a damn thing about making cheese. I'm new at it. And I'm taking this triple cream up there like the Holy Grail . . . and she's got her microscopes," he tells us. "And she says, 'Do you mind if I taste?' and she looks around [Chef Folse peers around conspiratorially] and says, 'I think this is just about the best cheese here. This is incredible cheese.'"

Chef Folse's Creole Cream Cheese, made from the milk of local Brown Swiss cows, has become so popular in Louisiana that it's being marketed throughout the country. In 2005, the American Cheese Society and *Saveur* magazine will give cheeses from Bittersweet Plantation Dairy top honors in their rankings.

At the time of our visit, however, actual goat cheese production is at least six months in the future, and though he claims to be an impatient man, Chef Folse is quick to say that he's willing to wait. Following McDonald around the milking parlor, he asks her questions about each piece of equipment, from the custom-designed chute that leads goats onto the milk stands, to the stanchions that hold their heads in place as they're being milked, exclaiming at the progress that's been made. Turning to us, he says it may seem like they're at the beginning, but "This is like we've just landed on the moon!" Though the building is a few months away from completion, the herd is nearly there.

Like other goat farmers we've met, McDonald is incredibly careful about her animal management, and as much as possible she's tried to expand the number of animals through her own breeding program instead of buying goats from other herds. Though this takes a bit longer, she tells us it allows her to breed the animals for desirable traits (heavy milk production, hardiness), cultivating the type of goat that will be most productive in her operation. Since the gestation period of a goat is only about five months, goats can be bred as many as three times in two years. Most births are at least twins, with a high proportion of triplets and a smattering of quadruplets, so even if half the births are male, the number of future milking does can double every kidding season. Lolling in the fallen leaves under the nut trees, the goats look oblivious to the fact that everyone is "biding their time for the girls to have their babies."

It's chilly as the four of us walk around the farm, and Chef Folse tells us that having grown up on a sugar plantation, he has a great respect for agriculture. But while he listens attentively to McDonald's discussion of breeding schedules, midnight births, and bottle feedings, he tells us he doesn't want to get into the dairy business. McDonald, on the other hand, loves the challenges of farming but has learned from experience that marketing goat's milk is another full-time job. Their partnership offers each of them the joys of their vocations but spares them the unwanted anxieties. As Chef Folse tells us, their model "might be a new look at American cheese making, where we don't all have to do everything. She doesn't necessarily have to make cheese, and I don't need to get into the dairy business." Their guarantee is mutual: she'll deliver great milk, and he'll buy it all.

Chef Folse's enthusiasm is infectious. His descriptions of the goat cheeses he's working on have us salivating, though in fact at the time of our visit none of them are perfected. They're still in research and development, but he describes them as if he were unwrapping them from their paper and spreading them before us on a cheese plate. He tells us, "People say, 'New Orleans, that's got to be exciting!'" And so each of his cheeses is steeped in the stories of the region, as well as its flavors. He'll make some fresh chèvre, but his focus will be on aged cheeses and triple creams (so named because they contain 75 percent or more butterfat). He tells us that his triple cream Evangeline, named for Longfellow's Acadian heroine, will be made of the richest milk, then aged several weeks until its rind is blooming and its center is almost molten. His Gabriel, named for the lost lover Evangeline seeks in Louisiana's swamps, will be wrapped in a fine vegetable ash, steeped in the bayou terroir, and aged even longer until it reaches absolute perfection. His goat butter will be creamy, tangy, and a little nutty—unlike any other butter, he says. The descriptions are so vivid that we can virtually taste them on our palates. They're imaginary cheeses, at this point, and perhaps because of that, they are perfect.

Before we leave, we can't resist asking Chef Folse about his audience with the pope. "So," we ask, "what did you cook for him?"

Chef Folse laughs, "Well, unfortunately I didn't serve him cheese."

A devout Catholic, he tells us he had been asked by the bishop of Baton Rouge to put together a meal representing the culinary heritage of the seven Creole nations for a visit the pontiff made to Louisiana in the mid-1980s. Unfortunately, the dinner was never held, but the Diocese of Baton Rouge assured Chef Folse that it would happen at some point. Several years later, Chef Folse was surprised by a call from Bishop Stanley Ott, inviting him to Rome to orchestrate a dinner for the conclave of bishops. "He said, 'Remember we were talking about that dinner with the pope? How would you like to do it?'" Folse says. "Every five years all of the bishops of the world have to go to the Vatican for a meeting with the Holy Father to get all of their instructions for the next five years, and it was on this occasion that they asked that I come over and do the dinner."

He put on an eight-course meal for the bishops, and the morning after, Chef Folse had a private Mass with the Holy Father, made him breakfast, and then sat and chatted with him at Castel Gandolfo for more than an hour. When we asked him what they'd talked about, Chef Folse said, among other things, sausage making. An avid hunter and fisherman before his elevation to the papacy, Pope John Paul II, like Chef John Folse, loved to experiment in the kitchen.

Chapter 10

Leaving Louisiana, we had planned to meander through Texas and Oklahoma before arriving at my mother's in Wichita for Christmas. In a brutally cold December, however, we end up making a direct line for Kansas, stopping only at a Motel 6 near Shreveport and at a *Roadfood*-recommended steakhouse in a gritty corner of rural Texas, where we enter through swinging saloon doors and I dare Karl to order the "lamb fries," a regional specialty of deep-fried lamb testicles. (He declines, and instead has smoked ribs and a side of fried corn on the cob, nails tapped into its ends as holders.) We arrive in Kansas late at night, several days ahead of schedule, and very cold. Though we've only been on the road for a few weeks, our feeling of relief at having a roof over our heads is intense; I can't think of a time that I've been more grateful for a warm bed.

The plan is for my mother to leave on her spring semester sabbatical a few days after Christmas. In her absence, we will take care of the house: pay the bills, forward her mail, and, if possible, clean out some overgrown gardens in the back. In return, we have—rent free—a centrally located base from which to launch our various travels.

Our first trip of the year will be a three-week excursion into the heart of Texas that we've planned for mid-January. We leave the day before Karl's thirty-fourth birthday, excited to visit the land of cowboys, ranchers, and meat goats. Home to the headquarters of the country's three Boer goat associations, the president of the American Meat Goat Association (AMGA), and many of the country's champion Boer bucks, the state is without question the center of the meat goat industry. Imagining our visit, we hold images of herders on horseback and vast flatlands teeming with beefy Boers.

The first stop, however, after a long day of driving, is the parking lot of an Austin Wal-Mart where we spend the night in the back of our car. In pouring rain, we crouch in the back and try to arrange our sleeping bags without opening the car doors, then sleep fitfully with the dog between us and awake to a muggy morning, looking disheveled and frizzy and feeling a little confused at being back on the road. Happy Birthday, Karl.

Our trip to Texas will mostly focus on the southernmost quarter of the state, the land of meat goats and formerly the heart of America's mohair industry. But our first destination is actually a visit with some cheese makers whom we arrange to meet in their stall at Austin's Westlake Farmers' Market, the largest producers' market in the state.

While for much of Western history, farmers' markets have been at the core of the urban experience—Les Halles in Paris was founded in 1185 and operated on the same spot for more than seven hundred years—in the United States, their importance is a relatively recent phenomenon. In the early 1970s, there were fewer than four hundred regular farmers' markets in existence, but since the passage of the Farmer-to-Consumer Direct Marketing Act of 1976 that encouraged their creation, local markets have proliferated. According to most counts, there are now more than three thousand. As people become more curious, and increasingly disconcerted, about the sources of their food, farmers' markets have cropped up in towns across the country.

Since the roots of our journey had been planted, to a degree, in the farmers' markets of New York City, in our travels we try to stop at as many of them as possible. The markets vary greatly between communities, picking up local flavors and enthusiasms: cheese curds in the upper Midwest, organic citrus in the South. In upstate New York, we visit one with about twenty stalls, selling edibles from ripe apricots and currants to heirloom beans to fresh dairy products, eggs, and meat. In Eugene, Oregon, the weekly market is made up of dozens, possibly hundreds, of vendors, offering everything from roasted hazelnuts to bitter leafy greens to organic clothing and funky felt hats.

In Austin, the Westlake Farmers' Market is somewhere in between, with fruits and vegetables, meats, prepared foods (Karl goes back several times to the flan booth), and goat cheese.

The goat cheese comes from Sara and Denny Bolton of Pure Luck Farm and Grade A Goat Dairy, which sits just outside of Austin in the Hill Country town of Dripping Springs. An organic farm and dairy, Pure Luck produces some incredibly sophisticated and widely acclaimed cheeses; in 2001, its Sainte-Maure, a strongly flavored, firm, aged log, covered with a light-beige crust and traditionally pierced through the center with a piece of straw, was awarded a blue ribbon by the American Cheese Society. Though they sell directly from a cooler on the farm (strictly by the honor system; there's a metal box full of loose bills to make change) and at stores across the country, the Boltons' most loyal customers find them each Saturday morning at the farmers' market. We find them surrounded by cheese samples under a white tent, Denny chatting with customers, Sara tactfully making sure they've paid for their cheese.

Arrayed around them are a smattering of Pure Luck's cheeses. The biggest sellers seem to be the fresh chèvres: heaped sample plates quickly diminish to crumbles of tangy plain, herbed parsley and garlic, and fresh basil pesto chèvre. Embracing the region—again, the notion of terroir—the Boltons offer other fresh cheeses that are flecked a deep red, blended with chipotle and Anaheim chili peppers. A generous mound of briny feta is offered from the next plate, while Sara's aged cheeses rotate through the samples: the famed Sainte-Maure is followed by a biting Claire de Lune, a cheese with a semi-firm texture but with the nutty, mushroomy flavor of Brie. As we stand beneath the tent, Pure Luck's award-winning Del Cielo, a creamy, ripened cheese similar to Camembert, whose name is Spanish for "from the heavens," makes several appearances among the samples. Each time it's out, I surreptitiously spear another toothpickful.

Though the day has begun misty, the parking lot where the market is set up is full of people with canvas bags, wandering the stalls for emu oil, organic pecans, salad greens, and, of course, cheese. A folksinger plays under one of the tents, and as we wander around the market, trying not to be underfoot in the Pure Luck tent, we see Denny break away for a moment from the clutch of customers to request a song. One line is about goats eating anything, and even though Denny protests loudly that it isn't true, he claps and shouts every time the word "goat" is sung.

When the Boltons met in the early eighties, Denny already knew Sara by reputation as a single mom with two girls and a few goats. Together they've become serious about their dairy—becoming Grade A, certifying their crops as organic, focusing on marketing around Austin—but it wasn't until five years earlier that Pure Luck cheeses broke onto the national scene. In competition, Pure Luck began receiving top awards, and with them the kind of recognition that led to a profile in Laura Werlin's book *The New American Cheese*. Now, their cheeses are regularly mentioned in articles and books about artisanal cheeses and are widely available in places as far away as New York's Artisanal Fromagerie and Bistro. Sara's cheese-making techniques, which she has taught in workshops at the dairy and in other regional venues, such as Langston University's Goat Field Day in Oklahoma, have taken her as far as Armenia, where she spent a month in 2002 visiting with cheese makers as part of a U. S. Agency for International Development (USAID) program.

At a certain point, things begin to slow, and we hover around the booth for the duration of the farmers' market, talking with Denny and Sara between customers. The majority of their week's business is done during this six-hour stretch every Saturday, and the two of them work as a team. Denny, tall, with a curly mop of hair and a robust, smiling presence, attracts customers and keeps multiple conversations flowing. Sara, diminutive and by her own account "a little like a Hobbit," keeps the cheese stocked and answers questions about the products. By early afternoon, the cash box is full, and they're running out of cheese. Denny runs several pieces over to various vendors, among whom there's a loose barter system.

When they've packed up their tent and the few logs of cheese that are left, we follow the Boltons from the market out to their farm, driving past countless ranches and live oaks through the hills of Texas as the weather gradually becomes wetter. By the time we reach the farm, it has gotten so muddy that Sara hops out of their van and recommends we park on the road to avoid getting stuck.

We slosh up to their house where, after leaving our shoes on the porch, we pad around and share a delicious organic salad made with their own greens, whole-grain bread, and some cookies that their daughter Hope made that morning with a friend who spent the night. During lunch, a car full of people pulls into the farm stand and gets stuck in the mud, so Denny puts on his shoes and a rain jacket and goes into the field to help pull them out. Sara's adult daughter, Amelia, who lives on the property and, with her mother, makes all the Pure Luck cheeses, comes by to meet us and have some lunch. A neighbor drops in for a visit and helps the family come up with a list of area goat farmers for us to contact. Everyone wishes Karl a happy birthday and much joy in the coming year.

Though we've just met them, we feel immediately accepted and embraced, like part of the Boltons' extended circle. We linger over tea for hours, our conversation ranging all over the place, talking about our future and their past.

Around five o'clock, as evening milking approaches, the rain stops, and we clomp through the sticky Texas muck to meet their herd and tour the dairy. The goats munch happily on hay and seek shelter beneath trees and sheds. When Sara enters the goat pen, they crowd around her tiny frame, and one puts its hooves on her as if to dance. In the nearby dairy, we take off our shoes again and are led through an incongruously white and tidy building that houses their cheese-making equipment and a climate-controlled room in which racks of creamy and pungent cheeses age. Their best, Sara explains, come from experiments, and she shows us various rounds of their latest works in progress, which are aging in an old refrigerator whose door is held on with a belt of twine. True farmers, they save everything, and Sara says that as long as it works, they'll keep using this fridge. It still makes us laugh to see award-winning cheeses stored in such a gypsy fashion.

It sounds melodramatic to talk about epiphanies on birthdays, or as the sky clears intermittently in rainbow weather, but talking to the Boltons and watching them with their family, Karl and I feel for the first time in our travels that we have found a model for the type of farm we envision for ourselves. Some animals, some vegetables, a modest life spent among those you love; this is all the fulfillment we want.

Sara and Denny's openness to ideas and to people is inspiring— in just a short day with them, we feel infused with a new energy and a sense that our goat dreams, like theirs, are possible to achieve. Their measure of success is on such a human and personal scale, that it spreads a whole new world before us. The feeling is hard to describe, but it is nearly physical, something like a flood of comfort through the blood, relaxing shoulders that are clenched from a night in the car, loosening limbs tensed with the nervous anticipation of three weeks on the road. We feel possibility rush through us like a drug.

Though it is still pouring rain when we gather our things to go, the light has turned a beautiful pale orange. It is as though, through the thundering clouds, the hills are glowing. Surrounded by goats and flourishing fields of vegetables, we feel we are not only in the heart of Texas but in its bosom. By the time we leave Pure Luck, warmed with tea but still a little damp, night has fallen and the sky has cleared. The stars are big and bright as promised.

Chapter 11

W
e travel through the gentle hills near Austin to the expansive grasslands of the southwest and farther to the stilled
buckles and waves of borderland desert, crowned by the
rusty crags of the Christmas Mountains. As we venture south, the
numbers of goats increase dramatically. From the road, we see herds
of them racing through the brush, sometimes being rounded up by
flanneled men on horseback, sometimes simply running, as though
excited or spooked by the wind.

Many are Angora goats, evidence of the mohair industry that,
until its government subsidy was eliminated in 1994, had been
prominent in the region. (Until the mid-nineties, the production of
mohair had been considered of vital importance to national security,
as for decades the fiber was widely used by the U.S. military. A large
government subsidy made it an attractive business prospect; rumor
in the goat world has it that before the subsidy's abolition, the largest
goat herd in America was owned as a side business by the Dow
Chemical Company.)

A large number of the goats we see from the road are part Boer, their genetics evidenced by the distinctive red-and-white coloring and stocky body shape of the breed. This is the part of the Texas goat industry that we've been anticipating: animals bred for meat in a state with a huge appetite for it. Our itinerary includes stops at several of the state's larger auction houses, and at two barbecue joints, both named Cooper's, where cabrito—goat meat barbecued on the bone in the Mexican style—is the specialty of the house.

Though I'm originally from nearby Kansas, I haven't spent much time in Texas, and Karl and I are both a little nervous as we go deeper into the state. It's so vast that it feels like we're in a different country. We have no idea what to expect, but our initial impression is one of incongruity. It is a state once governed by the current president, but it also elected Ann Richards. It's predominantly evangelical Christian, but it also embraces Kinky Friedman and Molly Ivins. We've been told that Texas is a "love it or hate it" kind of place, that our feelings about it will be sudden and strong. "What if we hate it?" I ask Karl. We're planning to spend three weeks here, but if that's the case, neither of us knows what we'll do.

Our first stop after Dripping Springs is Junction. The town of Junction, about two hours west of Austin, is small (population 2,618), rural, and ringed by scrubby bluffs of crumbly yellow dirt. Every Monday, it holds one of the largest goat and sheep auctions in the state. Approaching the auction house, we have little idea of its scale, but on the morning we visit about fifteen hundred animals will pass through its ring. Out back, we see acres of pens webbed by catwalks, containing thousands of animals; pulling his trailer behind a battered pickup truck, a man in chaps and a broad Stetson steps down. I try not to stare and then can't help blushing when he tips his hat to me before unloading goats for the day's sale.

Held in an unassuming building—it looks like a high school gymnasium with a 1950s-style coffee shop in the front—the auction draws bidders from across the country and all walks of life. On the cinder-block wall of the entranceway, a Spanish-language notice is tacked next to a calendar of major Muslim holidays. We're a little surprised by the democracy of the auction house, but it's a business, and regardless of one's personal beliefs and suspicions, we suppose, the key to this business is facilitating livestock sales. It's also in Texas, and as we will learn, Texas is a very democratic—small *d*—place.

The auction ring itself is compact, housed in a windowless room arranged like a theater. Sitting inside are a collection of Anglo and Mexican cowboys. With them is also a strangely androgynous and somewhat belligerent Native American livestock dealer. Dripping with silver and turquoise and sporting waist-length hair and long, talonlike fingernails, he threatens Karl with a lawsuit if he takes his picture. Pulling out his cell phone, the man scrolls down numbers and ostentatiously highlights his attorney's. I whisper to Karl that clearly the man is crazy or doing something illegal; Karl surreptitiously snaps a photo.

Sitting farther back among the buyers, near where I've perched with my notebook in the middle of the seats, are Levent Demirgil and Yuksol Pece of the Al Marwa Halal Meat and Meat Product Company. Levent and Yuksol, two Turkish Muslims from the New York area (Levent lives in New Jersey, Yuksol in Brooklyn), have flown to San Antonio, rented a car, and driven to this auction in hopes of buying eight hundred animals.

The men rarely need this many animals, we learn later, talking with them around the U-shaped counter of the auction-house café, but the first of February 2004 is the Id al-Adha, the Islamic holiday of sacrifice commemorating the near immolation of Isaac by his father,

Abraham. It is the duty of each Muslim family to buy a live sheep or goat, and depending upon their inclination, to either slaughter it themselves or hire a proxy to perform the sacrifice, after which the animal is eaten. Because their business is in an urban area, which doesn't easily lend itself to ritual animal slaughter, Levent and Yuksol expect to do most of the butchering, but they still need to buy unblemished zabiha animals, since each customer will inspect and choose a living sheep or goat.

As we look more closely at the group of buyers, we see that there are actually three or four Muslim men at the auction, distinguishable from the other bidders by their pressed slacks and shirts, loafers, and bare heads. They are scattered among the armchairs of the ring's first rows, interspersed among the flannel-clad cowboys and heavily made-up women; everyone—Muslims, cowboys, callers—is chain-smoking. (Everyone, that is, except Levent, who explains that he quit smoking when he got married so that he wouldn't annoy his wife.)

Sitting on the cement platforms of the back rows, Karl and I watch the action unfold. As in the pre-Ramadan sale we'd attended in Maine and the weekly auction we'd seen in Alabama, the animals are led into the ring for display while a fast-talking caller notes their features and acknowledges bids. Unlike the other sales we've seen, this one is all business—no instructions are given, no animals are sold as pets, no jokes or smiles infuse the scene with levity.

Two hours into the auction, after we've become acquainted with Yuksol and Levent, they tell us that the prices here are consistently too high for Al Marwa. On the phone with an associate at the New Holland auctions in Pennsylvania, Levent has learned that there, sheep and goats are going for almost ten cents less per pound, and the transportation costs would be a fraction of what they would pay from Texas. He's instructed the man to buy in Pennsylvania, and he and Yuksol gather their things to leave Junction. On their way out they stop for another cup of coffee, and we catch up with them.

Perched on low plastic stools, drinking bottomless cups of weak coffee, we order doughnuts and ask them their plans.

"We think there is a man in Uvalde who can help us," Levent tells us, "He has three thousand goats."

They have a tip from someone at the auction that about one hundred miles to the south there's a man with a substantial herd who might be willing to deal directly with Al Marwa rather than sending the animals through auction. From the coffee shop, where the waitress offers a horrified Levent a pork chop, they call the man from a cell phone and make an appointment to meet him later in the afternoon. We ask if we can tag along, and they agree but on the condition that Karl drive the lead car.

"We drive maybe too fast," Yuksol says, with an apologetic smile.

We're done with the auction and they're planning to leave in an hour, so in the interim Karl and I decide to try the first Cooper's barbecue on our list, located just a little way down the road from the auction house. From both the outside and the inside, the building is nondescript—its peaked roof and plate-glass windows could have housed any small-town steakhouse or even a chain restaurant. Inside, the decor is practically a caricature of the region: a ledge around the high ceilings is decorated with wagon wheels, mounted horns, and cattle yokes. We hang back at the entrance, trying to figure out the system, then pick up some plastic trays and make our way through a cafeteria line of roasted meats. Behind glass, like a deli counter, great pans of brisket, ribs, and cabrito are warmed by red heat lamps. Wordlessly, we point to the joints we want, and a server picks them up with tongs and hands us our plates. With all the meat, sides of vegetables seem superfluous, almost funny, but somehow we end up with paper cups of coleslaw and beans. On a counter, several degrees of sauce can be ladled from large vats, and huge tanks of plain and sweet tea sit next to stacks of Styrofoam cups.

Unlike the barbecued goat meat we'd had in Tennessee, this meat, while tender, stays on the bone. Its texture is a little fibrous, like that of beef brisket, and its flavor, though mildly goaty, is mostly of smoke and spice. Karl has a leg, and I have some ribs, the flat, sharp bones poking out of the meat like a rack of lamb. The portions are enormous—too much for us, really—but after watching the auction, we force ourselves to finish, out of respect for the animals.

At the appointed time, we meet up with Yuksol and Levent again outside the auction house, memorizing their silver rental sedan in case we are separated. On our road atlas, Uvalde looks like a major town (its name is in bold red and it has an entire county named for it), but getting there from Junction takes us down patched single-lane highways and through miles of empty fields. Even I, raised on the Kansas prairie, feel a touch of agoraphobia.

After about an hour and a half, we reach Uvalde where Levent, whose cell phone is briefly getting no service, stops at a gas station to call for directions to the ranch. Twenty minutes later, when our two cars pull up to a modest split-level home, we all realize that Levent has been misinformed. Dink Turner, a weathered rancher with decades of experience in the goat industry, has sold most of his herd and at present keeps only about three hundred goats. Of those, fewer than one hundred would satisfy the criteria that Al Marwa needs to fill: either the animals are too small, too large, too bred, or too castrated for the Id al-Adha market. Dink uses Levent's cell phone to call some other local ranchers (Levent stands by helplessly after surrendering the phone), but no one has the numbers to fill the Turks' needs.

Before leaving the Turner ranch, we arrange to see Yuksol and Levent again the following day at Producers Livestock Auction in San Angelo where they hope to have better luck. Our drive takes us through Rock Springs, a name that we can't place, though it conjures a vague recognition. From the car window, driving down the town's main street, we peer into the open doors of immense warehouses, filled to the ceiling with burlap sacks of mohair. The same is true in small towns throughout the region: this is Angora goat country. But the goats we pass on the side of the road all seem to have some Boer in them, their bodies stockier and fleshed out beneath great Angora capes. The ranchers, it seems, are keeping pace with the market, making the transition from fiber to meat animals.

Twenty miles down the road, it comes to us. "Taylor Botts!" I shout, startling Karl and Godfrey. Rock Springs, Texas, was the original home of Talib Islam, the cleric in Maine.

Producers Livestock Auction holds the largest sheep and goat auction in the country, with close to half a million animals passing through its ring each year. On this Tuesday morning, 9,500 goats and sheep are slated for auction, more in a day than most houses sell their entire year.

The Producers' auction house is by far the most sophisticated we visit. Though its decor is dated, the building is almost luxurious, with couches and wood-partitioned phone booths in the main hall, and an upstairs level with conference rooms and offices. To the left of the entrance is the Stockman's Café, a reasonably priced restaurant with cheerful waitresses and freshly made, improbably good food. The auction ring, which is situated to the right of the hall, is spacious with comfortable seats, plenty of leg room, and next to each chair, a tin can for cigarette butts and chew spit. Closed phone booths line one wall, and through a door, the stockyards stretch as far as the eye can see. Spanned with an extensive network of catwalks, the pens are efficiently organized so that each group of animals can be easily herded from the farthest corner into the ring.

By the time we arrive, around ten in the morning, the auction has been under way for several hours. Levent and Yuksol are still getting a feel for the place and have yet to bid, but animals are passing quickly through the ring.

Each group of goats or sheep is led by a "Judas" goat, so named because it betrays its own kind by leading animals into the ring and at times to the slaughter. (Karl and I figure out that it was a Judas goat that his parents' Canadian guest told us about on Thanksgiving.) As the auctioneer calls out the bids, one or two Judas goats are released from their ringside pen. They make their way through the wide door to a pen behind the building, where they herd the animals and lead them out through a series of chutes onto the sawdust.

The buyers are much the same as the day before, though there are two or three times as many. As at Junction, a couple of them seem to buy as many animals as they can, no matter their condition, while others are careful, asking the handlers to pull out certain animals so that they can get a better look. There are several other Muslim men at the auction, regulars who are referred to as "the Moroccan" and "the Egyptian." Some bid vigorously while some wait, as the men from Al Marwa do, until the animals are gathered in larger lots, which, from our untrained appraisal, seems to lower the price.

After a smoky hour watching the bids, Karl and I go out the back door to look at the stockyards. It's incredible: pen after pen after pen, each filled with animals of like characteristics that munch on hay and try to nose through the ice that has covered their troughs, oblivious to their fate. Every so often, a pen is empty, or holds an incongruous animal like a bull or horse. Two pens hold the gnarled stumps of bleached trees, on which black birds perch by the hundreds.

Standing on the catwalk, we're able to look down on the proceedings, as handlers move goats and sheep between pens, flapping a Wal-Mart bag on the end of a long stick to get their attention. Some goats hop over each other and try to climb onto each other's backs; the sheep, for the most part, scurry nervously and then huddle into a corner of their pen.

In such an organized format, and in such great numbers, goats for the first time become livestock to us, distinguishable from cattle merely by size. The meat goat industry, which had seemed a somewhat nebulous idea, is before us, mapped on the grid of the stockyards. This inner transition is overwhelming, so distant from the comfort of small cheese operations and bottle-fed kids. It's the antithesis of the lifestyle Karl and I are seeking, it's considering the animals as simply chattel. We look at each other, look at the pens, and shake our heads. We know in that moment that however we've toyed with the idea, we can never raise goats exclusively for their meat.

Inside, Levent and Yuksol have begun bidding, and by the end of the afternoon they've bought about three hundred animals. Though this is less than half of their projected number, they seem happy with the purchase, and when we leave them that evening, they have begun searching for a truck to bring them to their plant in Pennsylvania.

This is the greatest difficulty of buying animals from a distance: transportation. Had Al Marwa arranged for a truck before they got to Texas, they would have been locked into buying a certain number of livestock. Having not made prior arrangements, though, they're now forced to scramble. The weather has been treacherous, dumping ice and snow across the Northeast, and truckers are understandably reluctant to make the drive. It's almost impossible for the Turks to find someone willing to haul their animals to New York.

We have an appointment the next morning to speak with Benny Cox, the goat and sheep manager at Producers. When we arrive at eight, Levent and Yuksol are in the Stockman's Café, circles under their eyes, drinking coffee and eating cookies—since the griddle had been used to fry the morning's ham and bacon, they aren't comfortable ordering anything cooked. Benny is trying to arrange a trailer for them and postpones our appointment until there's resolution.

Word has spread about their plight, and cowboys in the café are sympathetic. As we join them for coffee, people wish the two men luck, and at one point a man in a vest and chaps touches his heart and says "Salaam aleikum." Levent and Yuksol look startled, but respond in kind.

"Since we left here last night," Levent tells us, "all we've done is try to find a truck. We've made phone calls—we even went to a trucker motel and put notes on the windshields of empty trailer cabs."

The two men are flying out of San Antonio at five, and as the morning progresses, they become more and more anxious. If no one can be found to transport the animals, they'll have to resell them from a distance at the next auction in San Angelo and will both lose money and return to New York with a fraction of the number of goats and sheep their customers need for the holiday.

Finally at noon Benny finds a friend of a friend who is willing to make the trip. At the eleventh hour, the Al Marwa goats and sheep are inspected, certified, and moved to the pens nearest the trailers. Levent and Yuksol look drained but relieved. Though their trip has been tense and at times frustrating, Levent tells us he's kept it in perspective. The Id al-Adha, for which these goats and sheep have been bought, commemorates sacrifice.

"Compared to Abraham," Levent says, "our trials in Texas were easy."

We've had a hunch and some anecdotal evidence, but Benny Cox has concrete figures that document the overall rise in demand for goat meat. In the past decade, he says, goats have gone from making up just 14 percent of his business to accounting for 51 percent. The demand for meat goats at Producers', the largest goat and sheep auction in the country, he reiterates, and consequently the world, now outstrips the demand for lamb. Leaving San Angelo, we head farther south to Sonora to talk about this shift with Marvin Shurley, president of the AMGA.

Long before we made it to Texas, we began hearing the name Marvin Shurley. When we had specific questions about meat goats, agricultural legislation, or changes in the goat industry, at least part of the answer was a suggestion that we really should "ask Marvin Shurley." Marvin has worked actively for the recognition of the goat industry as a commercial entity. He has gone to Washington and spoken with members of Congress, he's testified before the World Trade Organization, and met with foreign ambassadors. Most important, he has made connections, and cultivated relationships of mutual respect, with fellow goat producers—and politicians—around the planet.

We meet Marvin at his ranch, turning through a mechanized gate just past Shurley Draw, a dry creek bed that runs beneath the highway. The Shurley family has been ranching this land since 1893 and has been in the goat industry for more than a century. Though in the past the land supported cattle, goats, and sheep, in 1994 Marvin anticipated the trends and shifted exclusively to Boer and Boer-cross goats. At the time it made financial sense, and he's not regretted the move. He now has about nine hundred goats (eighteen hundred if you count the kids) on about four thousand acres and supplements the income they bring in with ventures into the burgeoning deer-hunting market and through the lease of rights to natural gas found under his pastures. With no mortgage on the land, varied sources of income, and savvy business skills, Marvin's is probably one of the most solvent enterprises we visit.

We stay the night in his guesthouse, a hunting lodge lined with taxidermied deer and prize goats, the smells of which drive Godfrey crazy all night. In the evening, we go with Marvin and his son Nick to a local steakhouse; though beef is on the menu, the business card is printed with a line drawing of a goat.

Over steaks we ask Marvin what he thinks is driving the increase in demand for goat meat, and he echoes what others have told us, that the rising affluence of immigrant populations—especially in the Northeast—has really spurred sales across the country. We tell him of our experiences with Yuksol and Levent, and he nods, saying, "That's exactly the kind of situation I'm talking about."

What he says makes a lot of sense. Because goat meat is the most widely consumed red meat on the planet, it only fits that in this peripatetic global community, people take their culinary preferences with them. His example of Thanksgiving is apt: "If you were living in another country, wouldn't you want a festive turkey for Thanksgiving?" Goats, especially roasted whole, are the turkeys of most of the world.

Marvin's greatest concern as the American meat goat market takes off, however, is the threat posed by imported meat. A tireless proponent of domestically produced goat meat, Marvin is worried that even as demand rises, American ranchers will not see profits. Despite the massive auctions we've seen, he tells us that the majority of goat meat consumed in this country is imported, mostly from New Zealand. Much of Marvin's work on behalf of the AMGA advocates legislation that would favor American goat ranchers. Even if this sort of regulation was to pass, Marvin realizes that American eating habits would also have to change if the goat industry were ever to rival that of beef, chicken, or pork. Of the 212 pounds of meat consumed annually by the average American, only two ounces is goat meat.

Leaving Marvin's, we head back to Kansas, stopping at the other Cooper's barbecue restaurant, Cooper's Old Time Pit Bar-B-Que in Llano, a town back in the Hill Country northwest of Austin.

Despite its humble setup, this Cooper's is sophisticated enough to have a Web site and mail-order business and a wall decorated with press clippings and photos of celebrities who've made the journey to eat there. *USA Today* has listed it as George W. Bush's favorite barbecue spot (his order? not cabrito but ribs), and it's been written up in countless publications, from *Roadfood* to *Texas Monthly* to the *Washington Post*.

Choosing meat from outdoor pits and ladling beans from big crocks lining the back walls on the inside, we find seats at long community tables, covered in red and white checkered oilcloth and packed with regulars—behind us are a group of men in camouflage jumpsuits the checkout women greet by name.

The cabrito, like all the meat they offer, is well seasoned and perfectly cooked, meltingly tender, and tenuously attached to the bone. The sauces are excellent, giving the meat a warm burn, and the side dishes are exactly as they should be—sweet cornbread, smoky beans, tangy coleslaw, and limitless cups of sweet tea. But I have a confession to make. By this point, having been on the road for three weeks, subsisting predominantly on goat meat, I am a little cabrito-ed out. I do eat some of Karl's goat haunch, but my own order is chicken.

Chapter 12

Back in Wichita, we spend several weeks regrouping—doing laundry, catching up on puppet orders, eating vegetables to balance out all the Texas meat. Our wedding is only six months away, so we also begin to firm up those plans.

Though we've decided on a date and location, the myriad details of the wedding—dress, caterer, music, rental goats—keep surprising us and proving difficult to arrange from a distance. My aunt Teri is making my wedding dress, and after a few forays into the world of bridal boutiques with their explosions of lace gloves and satin shoes, we decide to combine several patterns into one of quiet simplicity: capped sleeves, A-line skirt, flat bow at the princess waist, all in matte white silk. We cross our fingers that the dress will come together easily because, looking at our goat schedule, Karl and I can only come through Kansas City for fittings twice in the next two months. Though from the bridal magazines I'm devouring, I know most brides find the dress to be a struggle, for me, at least in theory, it's the easiest part.

Everything else in the wedding planning becomes a leap of faith. In my mother's kitchen, Karl and I listen to abridged music samples from Maine bluegrass bands on the Internet and try to imagine flavors based on e-mailed caterers' menus. We rent a yellow and white striped tent, port-o-potties, and two live goats, which we hope will be healthy, clean, and relatively well behaved. With Leslie Oster, our caterer, we tentatively plan a meal that includes smoked salmon, fresh seasonal vegetables, and, of course, local goat cheeses. In the middle of the night, I remember our coastal location and decide on a whim to check the tidal charts. The blood drains from my head; I feel dizzy. From the other room where Karl is in bed reading, he hears a low, moaning whimper.

"The tide," I mumble, when he comes to check up on me. "The tide . . ." I point to the computer screen.

Unless we move everything back several hours, we'll be married at low tide and our ceremony and light luncheon will stink of fish.

By the end of the month, we're ready to stop thinking about the wedding and get back on the road. Our next trips will take us north to Indiana, Illinois, Wisconsin, and Minnesota, and although spring has come to Kansas, in the upper Midwest we anticipate cold temperatures and the possibility of snow. We'll ease our way into it, however, by making our first stop at Capriole, Inc., in Greenville, Indiana, just over the Kentucky border.

We had first heard of Judy Schad and her Capriole cheeses the previous August from Max McCalman. He had included her Mont St. Francis on the cheese plate he put together for us and sang the praises of her Wabash Cannonball, which in 1995 was voted the American Cheese Society's Best of Show. Over the years, many of her cheeses have been award winners, and since the 1980s Judy has been one of a core group of women who've shepherded the movement toward American artisanal cheeses. Max put her at the top of his list of

American cheese makers and said that in the course of our travels we would be negligent if we didn't make a trip to her farm.

Approaching Greenville, which is located in a region called Kentuckiana, the area feels more southern than midwestern. Rather than the cornfields of northern Indiana with their slant toward Chicago, the topography here is rolling and hilly and the closest city is Louisville. There is a sense of the gracious South about the farm; Judy, in her cheese-making coat and farm slacks, meets us wearing a strand of pearls.

Because of some miscommunication, Judy had expected us the previous afternoon, so as Karl and I introduce ourselves we feel sheepish and a little at a deficit. We're not sure why—perhaps it's this initial confusion, or the fact that she's a cheese world celebrity—but as we unload Karl's cameras and ready my notebooks, we're both a little shy.

A writer and former doctoral candidate in Renaissance literature, Judy approaches cheese making with the whimsy of a poet and the rigor of an academic. In 1976, she and her husband, Larry, moved to the country to get back to the land, and since their property held a barn, they bought livestock to fill it. She began to experiment with cheese in 1982 after discovering that she didn't like to cook with the milk her goats were producing. Once she'd mastered the techniques of fresh cheeses, Judy became interested in aged ones, fiddling around until she'd found flavors and textures that she liked. She studied various techniques and traveled extensively, shadowing French cheese makers, learning to work with different bacteria and molds, and forming her own preferences for the results.

In the late 1980s she became friends—in part through ADGA—with a small group of women cheese makers who were scattered across the country but united by their common love of goats and cheese. These women included Mary Keehn, Jennifer Bice, Ann Topham, Mary Doerr, and Laura Chenel, names that now signify the "mothers of the American artisanal cheese movement." The women traded experiences and offered each other advice, meeting at conferences and organizing cheese-related trips around the country and across the globe. In an interview for Laura Schenone's book, *A Thousand Years over a Hot Stove* (Judy gives us a copy, her pages marked with tufts of the excelsior she uses to pack her cheese for shipment), Judy likened her relationship with these women to the early history of cheese making. "We had to talk to each other. There was no place in the United States to go and learn. You had to figure it out by trial and error. We just threw out a lot of cheese."

In the process, they honed their skills and created a vast array of specifically American cheeses, each incorporating the distinctive flavors of their respective regions. Today, Judy's cheeses include more than a dozen varieties, spanning the palate from mild to pungent. Their rinds vary from softly wrinkled to washed, their textures may range from creamy to firm. While fresh chèvre is made from pasteurized milk, the aged cheeses are often made from raw. But she learned from the French about the importance of terroir, and within each cheese the flavors distinctly reflect Kentuckiana either in name or ingredients. Two cheeses incorporate local bourbon; one of which, the O'Bannon, named for former Indiana governor Frank O'Bannon, is a variation on the French *banon*, which is wrapped in chestnut leaves cured in eau-de-vie. Judy ages her cheese in chestnut leaves soaked in bourbon. The Wabash Cannonball is named for the regional train line made famous by a Depression-era folk song popularized by The Carter Family and Roy Acuff.

Like many cheese makers we've met, once we've spent some time with her Judy is eager to share both her cheese and her knowledge. In her small farm shop, she pulls together a cheese plate that includes wedges of O'Bannon, Piper's Pyramid, Sofia, Old Kentucky Tomme, and Mont St. Francis, complemented by the delicious tang of pear *mostarda* and strawberry balsamic compote. The cheeses are spectacular, each so different that we can scarcely believe that they came from the same milk and are made by the same hands in the same cheese room.

The slightly grainy paste of the Sofia, a ripened chèvre marbled with ash, is wrapped in a soft, gray, speckled coat. It's a quiet cheese, sweet and lush in the mouth. The O'Bannon, in contrast, is firm and sharp, announcing itself with an alcoholic whiff as it's unwrapped. A white round is revealed beneath a flower of chestnut leaves, and with every bite, a liberal splash of bourbon washes across the palate. The Mont St. Francis, which we'd sampled at Picholine, this time impresses us with a strange alchemy in the mouth that shifts the cheese from nose-curling pungency to a mellow memory on the tongue. The spicy sweetness of the mostarda and the rich, fruity, almost floral taste of the compote enliven our mouths between cheeses; the strength of the flavors would overwhelm us if we ate them together. These tastes greet us before we even begin to look around the farm, introducing our palates to the place before our other senses catch up.

A little later, while giving us a tour of her Alpine goats, barns, cheese plant, and aging rooms, Judy speaks passionately about the need to remind oneself of terroir, that every food is rooted in the land. Over a dinner, funnily enough, of lamb chops—knowing we're on the road, the Schads generously and unexpectedly invite us to stay the night in the guest room of their restored farmhouse—the four of us talk about the need to slow down in general and, specifically, to make food once more the center of social life.

The idea that the pace of our lives had become too quick was one of the forces driving our project, taking us out of New York and into our agrarian dreams, but somehow, perhaps because we're in perpetual motion on the road, the notion is still somewhat abstract to us. It isn't until dinner with Judy—discussing the work of her friend, the poet and agricultural activist Wendell Berry, and the Slow Food movement, of which she is an active member—that we truly connect the forces guiding our choices with a concrete set of ideals. We don't simply want to make goat cheese. Rather, we want to center our lives around something both great and simple: producing food and devoting our lives to the pursuit and cultivation of real flavor, in every meaning of that word. Connecting the palate to the place suddenly seems the most perfect goal of our lives.

Some of this epiphany may be due to Larry Schad's excellent wine cellar. Some may be rooted in the language of Wendell Berry, whose books Judy lends us for the evening. Much, I think, is due to the "Slow Food International Manifesto," written by the Italian food activist and advocate Carlo Petrini, which condenses and articulates the somewhat amorphous thoughts we are having.

The Slow Food movement grew out of a protest organized by Petrini in 1986, when a McDonald's was built near the Spanish Steps in Rome. Speaking out against the prevalence of fast food and the quickening pace of life, Petrini and his supporters ate bowls of penne in front of the construction site. Conceived as the antithesis of fast food, Slow Food proposed a general slowing down, a conscious choice to create time in one's life to nurture the senses and savor the pleasures of the table. Advocating traditional recipes and indigenous foodstuffs, the organization encourages people to eat local foods in their seasons, and to make a conscious effort to support sustainable and ecologically sound methods of agriculture. The group is an intersection of high gastronomic culture and the most basic earthbound practicalities—eat what grows near you, and make it delicious.

Over the past two decades, Petrini's ideas have taken root, first in Europe and now worldwide. Currently there are more than eighty thousand members of Slow Food, and the organization supports Web sites, publications, and local *convivia*, or chapters, across the globe. Annual and biannual international festivals, mostly held in Italy, celebrate food producers around the world. The conference Terra Madre, held in a former Fiat factory in Turin, celebrates global food traditions and provides stipends to promote the attendance of farmers from the Andes to the Anatolian peninsula. Cheese!, held in Petrini's hometown of Bra, brings together cheese makers from all over the world, and invites participants to sample cheeses made with a variety of techniques—coagulated with pig's rennet, aged in a Tibetan cave, shaped like pastries into intricately patterned nuggets. In addition to these larger festivals, each convivium organizes its own events, from tastings to farm tours to celebrations of local foods. On a more political front, the movement advocates for sustainable methods of agriculture and especially for the preservation of traditional foods: heirloom seeds, heritage breeds of livestock, historical recipes.

The instant resonance of the articulated Slow Food ideals gives Karl and me a new focus for our exploration of the goat world. It feels as though that community has suddenly become more expansive, encompassing all of our interests and folding them into one larger philosophy. Through goats, we can address our political, historical, anthropological, and gastronomic concerns.

As Judy is finishing her morning milking and we're preparing to leave (hastily, after Godfrey has growled at her pet corgi and peed on her sunroom floor), she recommends that we visit Sofia Solomon in Chicago to get an idea of how cheeses should be treated. Sofia is one of Chicago's foremost purveyors of fine foods and wines; her company supplies cheeses and specialty foods to the top restaurants and retailers in the area. Judy holds her in such high esteem that she has named a cheese in her honor—the lightly aged, ash-laced Sofia—so we call to arrange a visit.

Searching for the address Sofia has given us on the phone, we don't know if we'll find her in a restaurant, a retail grocer's, or an office building. A sudden thunderstorm has burst over the city, coloring it a strange purple and obscuring the building numbers. Wending our way through a maze of cobbled streets and gentrified industrial buildings, we nearly miss the office. Damp and bedraggled, we ring a buzzer for Tekla, Inc., the business Sofia tells us she named for her mother, and are ushered into a warehouse, stacked to the ceiling with balsamic vinegars, imported oils, and preserved fruits.

Sofia, a trim, blond woman looking polished in a casual black pantsuit, introduces herself, warmly welcomes us, and motions us to a reception area near her desk. She seems utterly unfazed by our appearance and promptly offers us champagne and a plate of cheeses and condiments. Coming in from a thoroughly wretched day of city driving and foul weather, nothing could be more restorative.

Tekla, Inc., was founded by Sofia and her late husband, Leonard, in the late 1970s. What has evolved from the original business of spirits and caviar—Sofia nostalgically tells us of running a finger around the inside rim of a caviar barrel, licking the dried, briny bits—is a wholesale business in gourmet foods of all descriptions. Since Tekla began to carry it in the 1990s, however, cheese has become Sofia's love. Like many we've met, as she educated herself on the subject she became passionate about it, and she continues to pass along this fervor to her customers. Many of the renowned restaurants in Chicago, including Avec, Tru, and Café Spiaggia, come to Sofia for their cheeses. Often she conducts mini-workshops, discussing different varieties and principles of cheese making with chefs and restaurant staff. In some cases, she organizes tastings for the chef; in others, she's given free rein to select trays for them from her caves. Most of the restaurants she works with rely on Sofia for their cheese's *affinage*, or aging, and in her two caves, she is continually assessing their ripeness in order to provide cheeses at the perfect moment.

Following her into various walk-in refrigerators—each kept to a specific temperature and humidity level—we are struck by the different characteristics of the cheeses. On some shelves, the same cheese is held at different stages of ripeness, and we can see on the rind the evolution of the mold. On other shelves, Sofia picks up cheeses and sniffs them in anticipation or disappointment, telling us that some are perfectly aged, while others are, alas, just past their prime. For the Chicago gourmand, much, we can see, depends on her nose.

Sitting down with her, we ask how she decides which cheeses to carry, and she tells us, a little conspiratorially, that although she deals primarily in French cheeses, she often finds American cheeses through the recommendations of rival cheese makers. Pointing to a bit of cheese she's given us to sample—a wonderful Vermont cow's milk cheese, pale, almost tangerine in color, tangy and firm like a cheddar, with a granular feel in the mouth—she confesses that it came to her attention by way of another cheese maker from New England.

"This loyalty," she says, is what she loves about American artisanal cheese makers. "They pay close attention to me, to their customers, and to each other."

Strangely, in the course of our discussion and tour of Tekla, we only briefly touch on the place of goats in the cheese pantheon. There is so much else to see and taste in this bliss of rarefied foods that we want to experience and savor every morsel, from the dried cakes of fruit to the roasted almonds and pistachios to the plump, sticky dates, and of course, the perfectly ripened cheeses.

As we're leaving, we remark on how wonderful it must be to come to work in this environment; though we dream of a life in the country, Tekla's warehouse would be a pretty close second. Gesturing to the room around her, Sofia smiles and declares simply, "We like what we do, and as Leonard used to say, we do eat and drink well."

In between our visits to Judy and Sofia, we make a slight detour to downtown Chicago. Under a train trestle, near the Wrigley Building and the Tribune Tower, sits the Billy Goat Tavern. Made nationally famous by Dan Akroyd and John Belushi's "Cheezborger, Cheezborger"

Saturday Night Live skits in the late 1970s, the tavern is a Windy City landmark because of its purported "Curse of the Billy Goat."

In 1945, a Chicago Cubs fan named William "Billy Goat" Sianis bought his pet goat a ticket to the World Series. The Cubs were facing the Detroit Tigers at Wrigley Field, and Sianis, an immigrant from the Greek village of Paleopyrgos, had spent $14.40 on tickets for two box seats to the game. He arrived with his goat, presented their tickets, and after some discussion was turned away by the management. When Sianis asked why, he was told that the team's owner, Mr. Wrigley, had objected because "the goat smelled."

What happened next is unclear. In some versions of the story, Mr. Sianis and his goat left the ballpark and returned, angry, to the Billy Goat Inn, a tavern he owned that had gotten its name after someone left a baby goat in a box on his doorstep. At the bar, Sianis is said to have told a newspaperman that his goat had been insulted and disappointed, and the Cubs would be hexed until Mr. Wrigley came to the tavern to apologize to the animal. In another version, man and goat stood outside Wrigley Field and Sianis raised his fist, shouting, "The Cubs no win here no more!" Whatever the duo's actions, the Cubs lost the game. The following day, Sianis sent Mr. Wrigley a telegram: "Who smells now?"

In the years that followed, the Billy Goat Inn has changed locations and name, moving in 1964 to its current address and becoming the Billy Goat Tavern. Four goats—Billy, Murphy, Sonoria, and Socrates— have split their time between Sianis's backyard and the tavern (though now the only goat to be found on the premises is mounted above the bar). The place and its proprietor have ascended to legend, immortalized in television and in print by Mike Royko of the *Chicago Tribune*. The bar has become a destination for politicians, journalists, and sportscasters. The Cubs have not returned to the World Series.

Sitting in the tavern in the late morning beneath the many photographs and laminated newspaper articles that line its walls, we ask

Billy Goat's nephew, Sam Sianis, a small man with a shock of white hair and a thick Greek accent, why the curse persists. By his own admission, he's been invited to bring a goat to Wrigley Field; what more needs to be done? He pauses for a moment in the din of the bar, which, even in the morning, bustles with people stopping in for coffee and egg and cheese sandwiches.

"There have been occasions," he tells us ominously, "when I've taken goats to Wrigley Field and they've still been turned away."

The first time was in 1973, when he and the goat arrived in a limousine but were refused entrance. The most recent was this past year, when Sam's goat had tickets to games six and seven of the playoffs but was prevented from entering. It is because of these rejections—the capriciousness of the Cubs, as it were—that the curse has not been broken.

Sam truly believes in the Curse of the Billy Goat, he tells us, and he believes that the only way to lift it is sincerity. The invitations that have been issued so far have been mere publicity stunts. If the Cubs opened the stands to goats because they genuinely liked them and wanted to share the game with them, the hex would be dispelled.

Oddly enough, Sam's sentiment—that above all, sincerity is what matters—echoes and reinforces the philosophical conclusions we've begun to draw from our talks with Judy and Sofia. Living an integrated and honest life, whether on a farm, in a cheese cave, or at a ballpark, is what brings these people joy and is what fuels them in every endeavor. An aspiration to this kind of life started us on our journey, and the reminders, in such different settings, bring new energy to our project. Though our focus was initially an exploration of the various roles of goats in America, we now begin thinking of them in the context—at the core—of our own lives. Rather than seeing goats as the question, we're starting to see them as the answer.

Chapter 13

Six months into the goat project, we feel as though we've learned a great deal about the animals and our intentions. We know that we do want to become goat farmers and, moreover, that we want to raise dairy animals rather than meat goats. Now, rather than simply looking for certain aspects of the goat world, we're trying to find models for an entire lifestyle. We want to see where we can fit in, and in addition to goats, we're seeking that same sincerity, that coherence of life and work, that animates Judy and Sofia and Sam, and that we found earlier in people like Max McCalman and Sara and Denny Bolton. What we want to see are the nuances of people's lives, the subtle differences between their farms.

After Chicago, and through the course of the spring, we visit farms across the upper Midwest. The rhythm of our travel is in some ways repetitive: we drive from farm to farm, stopping at dozens to tour their barns and pens and milking parlors. We talk to old-timers who've been in the goat business for generations, former back-to-the-landers, and farmers just barely more seasoned than we are.

We've learned a lot about goat care and management, though our education is all from study not practice. But we can carry on a conversation about goats with fluency, and that feels like an achievement.

We can also make jokes. Visiting Earl and Marge Kitchen, the goat collectible vendors from the ADGA convention, at their home in Grandy, Minnesota, we find goats in every corner, from the hundreds of Bock beer bottles lining the walls of their guest room to the embroidered goat hand towels to the painted Russian *gzhel* ceramic figurines. Over dinner with their friend Karyl Dronen, the three tell us about a trip they took to France. In Paris, Marge says, it seemed like all the women except the two of them were pregnant.

"It must have been kidding season," I blurt, and then wonder if I've said the wrong thing; I'm insecure, as though I've told a joke in a foreign language. Marge and Karyl look at me for a moment and then burst out laughing, Marge clapping her hands and slapping the table, saying, "Margaret, that's a good one!"

I'm euphoric, beaming—not only do I get the goat jokes, but I make them! It's a moment of pure joy.

In Scandia, Minnesota, at the recommendation of Marge and Earl, we make our way to Poplar Hill Dairy Goat Farm. Owned by Vince and Christine Maefsky, Poplar Hill is the largest commercial dairy we visit, about three times the size of Split Creek. Milking nine hundred goats twice a day, they take shifts of forty-eight does into their sunken milking parlor. We can see immediately that the scale is too large for us. Standing at its edge, looking down on the machinery that methodically pumps each goat's teats, I whisper to Karl, "Each milking shift is larger than most of the herds we've seen."

Vince and Christine began their immersion in the world of goats in the early 1970s in an intentional community of young, politically liberal Catholics, where they had one beloved milking doe named Dorothy Day after the founder of the Catholic Workers Union. In photographs they show us from that time in their lives, the two of them sit in a smiling clutch of idealistic-looking young men and women—all beards and pigtails—scratching the goat at their center. At the time, Vince, a former seminarian, was a conscientious objector to the Vietnam War and was sent to do his alternative service in rural Minnesota, far from extended family and friends. Christine, a children's educator who studied at Columbia University, followed in a Volkswagen packed full of chickens, and by 1972 an embryonic Poplar Hill Dairy Goat Farm was formed.

Now, in an office lined with ribbons and trophies from goat competitions and samples of a new milk carton design, the two talk about the satisfaction of running a family farm. In three decades its scale has grown—"Yes," Christine admits, "we've had to sacrifice some of the intimacy with the animals." But they work together, and their children work with them, and growing the business together as a family has been satisfying for them all.

Karl and I can imagine the gratification of a family farm, and touring the property, we can see why their children stay. Poplar Hill is a trim, well-maintained collection of buildings and pastures in the midst of some woods set along a small lake. Its surrounding fields provide much of the farm's feed, and when we visit, the earth is turned over and ready to be sown with this year's seeds. Vince drives the four of us around in an open all-terrain vehicle, bouncing down the rutted farm lanes and pointing out his corn cribs, a restored barn that the family has recently reshingled by hand, and past saplings and some precariously gnawed tree trunks, the lake's especially large beaver dam. It is idyllic, on a grand scale but designed along cozy midwestern lines. The long barns, each housing hundreds of does, are red and white; the pastures, to which the goats have ready access, are tinged with the bright green of early spring. It's strange, but on this scale it's almost hard to believe that the farm houses goats. With all of its resources, space, and self-sufficiency, it seems more like the classic picture of an American cow dairy, an image from the panels of a turn-of-the-century quilt.

In a part of the country that was once dotted with small, well-groomed family farms, it is increasingly difficult to make a living in small-scale agriculture. Farms like the Maefskys', which are large by goat standards but modest by others, are few and far between. Especially in the dairy business—even more so in cow dairies than goat—it's become almost impossible to compete with the immense "factory farms" of agribusiness. Without finding a niche like organic milk, returnable glass bottles, or cream on the top, family farms can't justify to the market the prices they must charge to stay afloat.

On the recommendation of Judy Schad, Karl and I have begun delving into books by Wendell Berry, notably *The Unsettling of America*, which traces the decline of family farming and the subsequent distancing of Americans from their food sources and the land. We've also brought Gary Paul Nabhan's *Coming Home to Eat* on the road with us, reading with amazement about his year eating only what could be found within a 250-mile radius of his desert home. The more Karl and I read about contemporary farming and agricultural policy, and the more we talk to farmers who are living within this context, the more important our food choices begin to seem.

"How did we not know this?" we wonder aloud, a little ashamed of our own ignorance. The desire to slow down our pace, grow our own food, and support other small farmers is no longer simply an attractive dream but a true imperative.

We are newly impassioned when we visit Ada Austin at her Angora farm and gift shop in the heart of southern Minnesota's Amish country. Arriving at her property late at night after Ada's gone to bed, we're directed by her husband to a corner of their fields near a dirt crossroads where we can camp for the night. Turning off the engine, we're exhausted and decide not even to pitch our tent, unrolling our sleeping bags in the back of the car and nestling the dog between us. My mind is wandering as I lean against a knotted old tree, emptying my bladder one last time before sleep.

Suddenly, I jump at a flash of lightning and a crack of thunder; in the distance, there's an approaching rumble and two voices singing. As orange sheet lightning illuminates the sky and heavy drops begin to splash through the branches, I struggle to pull up my pajama bottoms and crouch down to hide as a black horse-drawn carriage flies down the road, its occupants laughing and harmonizing as they try to beat the rain. It's a surreal sight, and in the quiet of the fields, Karl and I are a little awestruck. Wound up on new adrenaline, we can't fall asleep and lie in our sleeping bags talking as rain pummels the car.

In the morning, we meet Ada, a pragmatic farmer with a head of wild white curls that match her Angora goats, a strong Minnesota accent, and a cheerful, earnest disposition. Her business is not in goat milk or meat but in handcrafted mohair products, which she buys from stay-at-home mothers in the region in hopes that it will allow them to supplement (or in some cases provide) the family income while caring for their children.

"A woman with her back to the wall is kind of scary," she says with a laugh. She's been there, and now it's her mission to channel that energy into craft. Her regional marketing savvy has brought her customers as diverse as the local Amish wives and the late King Hussein of Jordan; he visited while receiving treatment at the nearby Mayo Clinic and bought mohair socks ("They're my bread and butter") for the entire Jordanian royal family. Of the king, Ada says, "He was just like your favorite uncle."

More than a businesswoman, however, Ada's a networker. She makes connections between women in the area, and before we leave her farm, she recommends that we visit single mother Joy Peckham in Cresco, Iowa, for a look at how the introduction of goats has once more made a family farm profitable. In Ada's opinion, "Goats just might save the American agricultural tradition."

Over the Iowa state line, down a rural route from which subdivision construction can be seen, Peckview Dairy is another reminder of what the midwestern landscape once looked like. Its tall, white farmhouse sits near the road beneath arching trees, while behind it long, low barns hem in the backyard and a pebbled drive before expanding into pasture. We knock on the door and are greeted by a broad woman with short brown hair and a no-nonsense manner. When she was growing up on the property, Joy tells us, her family raised dairy cows, and there's still a sign leaning against the barn that reads "Peckham Holsteins."

"We were a fourth-generation Holstein farm, but I couldn't make ends meet with the cows," Joy tells us. Much to her family's surprise, with goats, she could. Now raising purebred Alpines, she tells us the animals make sense to her: their size is manageable for a woman to control, they use her resources efficiently, and the market for their milk is growing. Also, their intelligence makes them much easier to manage than cows.

Several times a week, the truck from a regional co-op collects her milk and takes it to a facility where some is bottled and some turned into cheese. In the summer, Joy sells some farmstead cheeses and fudge of her own at the local farmers' market, but her steady income, she says, comes from the fluid milk.

"My brother thought it was weird," Joy says, "switching to goats. They're still kind of an 'alternative' livestock around here." But raising her three children on a farm and giving them a similar upbringing to her own kept her motivated to do whatever she could to keep the farm in production. Gesturing to the development going on just over her property line, she says that no matter what animals they raise, she'd rather her kids grow up on a farm than in one of the encroaching suburbs. Raising dairy goats has made this possible.

The new commercial viability of dairy goats is something we talk about with Harvey Considine, member emeritus of ADGA and father of the organization's current president. A ruddy man in a tweed cap with a mild Irish brogue whose office is lined with photographs and memorabilia from both the local and national Republican parties, Harvey seems an unlikely progressive. He's rural, politically conservative, and an evangelical Christian. Yet in more than fifty years in the goat business, he's helped to shape the structure of ADGA, worked hard to promote dairy goats, and made his farm in Portage, Wisconsin, a hub of goat activity. The father of twelve, Harvey is also the progenitor of something of a goat world dynasty—six of his children raise goats, judge goat shows, and are intensely involved in the workings of ADGA.

Though he's officially retired from farming, Harvey and his wife, Elaine, continue to live on their farm in a house they've built for retirement. An older farmhouse, closer to the barns, is inhabited by Harvey's son Tom and his family, who are currently farming the land. Harvey continues to appraise goat herds and stays active in the goat community ("My hand can just touch an udder and know if it's healthy"), but he's slowed down his pace, focusing instead on his grandchildren and his hobbies: a small orchard of various fruit trees and a business making goat-leather thimbles. Though we've come to see the goats, he leads us through his orchard and gardens, the trees beginning to bloom sweetly, fat green tips of asparagus nosing their way through the earth. "Goats were the first love of my life," he says, "horticulture was my second."

Later, in his living room, with a mallet and a set of leatherworking tools, he demonstrates for us his thimble-making technique, pounding and stretching the cured goat skin on the coffee table as his wife looks on indulgently.

Having been involved in the goat world for half a century, Harvey has witnessed many changes. Most noticeably, he's watched as dairy goats and their milk made a shift from the margins to the fore-front of local family farms. "You have to treat your farm like a busi-ness. It can't be a question of how slowly you'll lose money, you're in it to make some," he says. "Here in Wisconsin cow country, people laughed at first when we got goats, but they stopped laughing when they saw the milk checks."

Harvey's explanation for the evolution of the dairy goat industry is easy, though it has nothing to do with the reasons we generally hear: goats' ubiquity, low environmental impact, versatility. Harvey says simply that goat people have always been independent thinkers, but now the rest of America is catching up and finally starting to rec-ognize their animals' qualities. The explanation he leaves us with is easy. As Harvey says, "Goats produce the finest milk, meat, and leather . . . that's goats."

Chapter 14

A t almost every stop we make in the Midwest, we're welcomed like family, and, when we leave, given little affectionate to-kens. Harvey Considine sends us on our way with a goatskin thimble (he's right, it does change the whole puppet-making experience) and a bag of frozen Queen Anne cherries from one of his trees. Joy Peckham offers us goat's milk fudge; Ada Austin makes sure we have warm socks. Though we arrive as virtual strangers, having made brief contact by e-mail or phone, we are treated with warmth as though we're part of an extended community. To a degree, this may be because of our interest in goats and our expressed resolution to try to promote the animal. When it's repeated in all corners, however, we begin to suspect that the congeniality of these farmers springs from something much deeper.

Before this leg of our journey, Karl and I hadn't given much thought to the ethos of the family farm, nor to the kind of connections and bonds it might forge. We were interested in goats, the people who raised them, and the larger community of the goat world. As we make our visits, however, especially to those farms where children are being raised, we begin to think about what it is emotionally that a family farm provides. Working together, eating together, living together: this is a combination that from our earlier perch in New York sounded claustrophobic and gave us anxiety about our own plans for the road. But watching the dynamic between members of families on working farms, our view is entirely changed.

Beginning with the Boltons in Dripping Springs, we start to see that kind of closeness as something both productive and positive, and our trip to the upper Midwest just reinforces these impressions. On a small working farm, everyone has a role, responsibilities, and, in larger terms, a place. People pitch in and help each other, knowing that every chore—however simple—is important. This isn't to say that living on a farm makes life's relationships easy, or that farm families are always cheerful, but on a very basic level it means that everyone engages with one another, in part because they don't have the luxury of hiding in their room with a laptop or XBox. There are animals to feed, eggs to collect, gardens to weed. And the people whose love and approval are most important depend on each family member to get this work done.

Karl and I both grew up in homes where chores were things like feeding the dog or making our beds. The only thing that depended on their accomplishment was, maybe, our allowance. The more farms we visit, though, the more we see that the fair delegation of real responsibility results in incredible family bonds. Watching families in action, we suspect that the feeling of urban disconnection that first led us to explore these farms might be completely eradicated by adopting this lifestyle.

Driving the long stretches of interstate, our daydreams and our conversations begin to shift. The more small family farms we visit, the more we talk about scaling down our ambition from a commercial goat operation and starting slowly, deciding in the large scheme how we truly want to shape our lives.

One visit that provides clarity for us is Antiquity Oaks, a small, diversified farm outside Joliet, Illinois. Owned by the Boehle family (pronounced "bay-lee"), the farm has a small herd of goats but more generally focuses on all types of heritage breeds of animals—endangered livestock that is threatened with extinction because it doesn't fit neatly into the large scale farming model.

Earlier in the year, we had learned a little about heritage breeds from Callene Rapp, a senior zookeeper at the Sedgwick County Zoo in Wichita. Walking around the zoo's livestock barn, Callene had explained to us that many of the animals we saw on display—immense Tamworth pigs, shaggy Scottish Highland cattle, affectionate Nigerian Dwarf goats, and even the myriad breeds of poultry—were becoming rare because their defining traits didn't conform to the needs of the contemporary meat and dairy industries.

"With current methods of commercial farming," she said, "animals are bred for short, productive lives. It's about quick weight gain and confinement."

Animals that don't fit into that plan aren't profitable, and their numbers have gradually dwindled. Though some farmers have taken an interest in the heritage breeds, their numbers are not large enough to successfully combat the problem; in some breeds, fewer than one hundred animals are now left.

While a few of these numbers have declined because of aggressive action, the populations of most endangered livestock breeds have dwindled in a passive way. When their product—generally meat—fails to turn a profit, they are phased out of their farmer's breeding program. Pigs that were once raised for their lard and found on nearly every small farm in America have decreased in numbers to a few hundred. Versatile cows that could provide milk and meat, or those like the Scottish Highland whose thick coats of fur encourage marbling in their beef, don't gain weight quickly enough or need too much exercise to be commercially viable.

"Since most people don't raise and slaughter their own livestock anymore," Callene laments, "entire breeds may be lost."

Before we left the zoo, Callene gave us a painting made by one of our favorite animals, a red Hereford pig named Lucille who is close to five feet tall and whose pointy ears stand erect and alert. When she's not rooting around in her stall, Lucille makes paintings with her snout; ours is an abstract work in reds, blues, and bits of corn.

Callene also turned us on to the American Livestock Breeds Conservancy (ALBC), a conservation group on whose board she serves. The ALBC was founded in 1977 and is dedicated to the preservation of historic breeds of livestock and their genetic lines. Organizing conferences and publishing a directory and newsletter, the group connects breeders and tracks populations of livestock that may be nearing extinction. Like any conservation group, its literature is full of watch lists, success stories, and cautionary tales. Unlike most conservation groups, however, it encourages members to eat many of the animals they are trying to preserve. The idea, while at first blush seems counterintuitive, is to develop a market for the meat of heritage livestock so that the animals will be bred more, have better genetic diversity, and eventually be taken out of the zoos and put back on the farm.

The ALBC opened our eyes to a whole new facet of American livestock, and we immediately became members. Several American goat breeds appear on their watch list—San Clemente, Myotonic, or "fainting" goats, even the registered dairy breeds of Oberhasli and Nigerian Dwarf. We had yet, however, to meet anyone other than a handful of dairy goat farmers who were raising these endangered animals, and no one who made decisions about their farm's animal breeds as a philosophical choice. No one, that is, until the Boehles.

As the name suggests, Antiquity Oaks looks to the past for its inspiration. The Boehles—Deborah and Mike and their children, Margaret, Jonathan, and Katherine—have consciously chosen to model their farm on a turn-of-the-century homestead, raising a varied collection of animals and vegetables for their own needs and consumption. Like early settlers in the area, they produce their own eggs, dairy products, and meat, and they grow and preserve fruits and vegetables.

Nestled in rolling, wooded farmland, their property is scattered with garden plots, fenced pastures, and ponds. Not far from the house, a barn contains their livestock, which at this time of year includes baby chicks, newborn goats, and two calves. The breeds they've chosen include Nigerian Dwarf goats, Irish Dexter cattle, Dorset Horn sheep, and a variety of brightly plumed chickens, ducks, and turkeys that freely wander throughout the property.

Talking with them, Karl and I realize that the Boehles are a few years ahead of us but on the same path. Deborah, a freelance writer and former journalist, and Mike, a professor of electrical engineering, made the decision to move to the country several years ago with great enthusiasm but little agricultural experience. In the years that followed, they've read extensively, found mentors across the Internet, and experimented with animal husbandry through a system of informed trial and error. Their children are homeschooled and participate in every aspect of farm life; for the whole family, the farm has provided a broad education.

Deborah, who began a graduate program in education at Brown University before realizing that she didn't want to teach in a classroom, considers the farm an ideal education. There the family works in collaboration, and lessons are learned not at a desk but in the barn. Fractions are taught by halving a cookie recipe, biology is learned asking questions of the vet. The kids are encouraged to pursue their curiosity, whether it leads them into a book or into a pasture.

These are not the kids we expected to find on a farm in rural Illinois. They are precocious and engaging, poised around adults, and really pleasant company. They know interesting things and readily share them in conversation. At the dinner table, over a meal of some extraordinarily plump chickens that they tell us were raised on the farm, the kids discuss politics and popular culture. Jonathan, a thirteen-year-old movie buff, asks Karl if he knows the work of Robert Altman; Katherine, ten, chimes in, "Isn't he the one who directed *M.A.S.H.*?"

The Boehles seem remarkably close knit and truly respectful of each other. They also seem to live with an intention that has developed organically. They are all devoted to making the farm work. It's both a collaboration and an education.

Food, discovering its origins and making moral decisions about what to eat, is a huge part of life at Antiquity Oaks. It is the kind of life lesson that is rarely taught in a meaningful way to young people, and we leave wondering if on a large scale some of the social ills that plague our culture couldn't be solved by reconnecting children with their food sources. The thought sounds both lofty and a little trite on paper, but the respect and gratitude that the Boehle kids obviously feel for their animals is anything but.

A woman we visited in Iowa told us about children from a rural grade school visiting her farm, and one of the questions put to her by a fourth-grade student was, "What kind of egg does a cow hatch from?" Seeing the possibilities at Antiquity Oaks makes this question all the more horrifying.

On the drive back to Kansas, Karl and I talk a lot about the idea of homesteading while fantasizing about the plants and animals we'd like to raise. We make lists of heirloom vegetables and try to realistically imagine ourselves raising a spectrum of animals. Admittedly in our enthusiasm our lists grow to unrealistic proportions, but our questions remain grounded. Could we slaughter our animals? Could we exist almost entirely from the literal fruits of our own labor? Our curiosity has been awakened to something broader than exclusively goats, something combining agriculture with conservation and education and a sort of activism by example. We want to believe that we're made of this strong stuff, that we could work together as (eventually) husband and wife, tilling the soil, milking the goats, and making of our lives something honest and true.

Chapter 15

Back in Kansas in the middle of spring, we're excited about the idea of homesteading, though in this part of the country, the word has a different, historical connotation of prairie, sod roofs, and dust bowls. Until now, we've resisted the phrase "back to the land," thinking of any label as a little hackneyed. We've also stayed away from it because we haven't felt as though we've joined a movement, and so often as we describe our project, it's been met with a dismissive: "You're way too late for the back-to-the-land movement—that was in the seventies, but it's been over for decades."

But what people like the Schads and the Maefskys and so many others sought in the seventies—a conscious slowing down and a deeper connection to the natural world—is exactly what Karl and I are looking for now.

Regrouping for a few weeks at my mother's, we practice that life, rising with the sun to spend our days working in the garden, baking bread, and doing household chores. We cut jonquils and tulips for the dining room table and have simple, homemade meals for dinner.

In the evenings we take walks through the neighborhood, read books about farming, and, endlessly, make goat puppets. In the middle of a medium-sized city, we create for ourselves a quiet life, and we find that even within urban limits it begins to satisfy us.

It's important that we fill up on domesticity now, because our next trip—into the vast West—will be our most ambitious. We'll be on the road for six weeks, driving through the Rockies, the desert, up the coast of California. After this adventure, and one final dress fitting, we'll head back east for the summer and, in August, our wedding. It's important that on this great western expedition, which will take us through America's largest concentration of goat cheese makers, we answer our lingering questions: can we really choose this kind of life? And if so, where?

Our first stop after the flat, expansive plain of western Kansas is outside Boulder, Colorado, in the town of Niwot. In the shadow of Haystack Mountain, we visit Jim Schott's Haystack Mountain Dairy, a farm and Grade A dairy that sells fresh and aged cheeses in the Denver area.

We had first discovered the dairy on the Internet when we were doing our early Web searches from our apartment in Brooklyn. We had just returned from our trip to South Africa, and finding that Jim had done volunteer work at a small South African dairy had felt like one of the cosmic signs nudging us out of New York and onto the road. Now, practically a year after first reading about him, we're anxious to make the connection.

Arriving at the farm late in the morning, Karl and I pass through an arch of trees lining the drive before reaching the main pastures and buildings. The farm, like many others we've visited, is an agricultural holdout in a sea of development, and on the sweep of meadow leading up to the mountains, new house construction can be seen in virtually all directions.

We've tasted some of Haystack Mountain Dairy's cheeses already; the lightly smoked chèvre is a surprising delight with the clean tang of fresh cheese followed by a lingering flavor of apple wood smoke. Beneath its soft rind, the aged Haystack Peak is creamy and dense, almost custardy in texture. The Queso de Mano, with a buttery yellow rind and a firm paste, is a little nutty; closing our eyes, there's an aftertaste reminiscent of green pastures.

Though his dairy has grown up around him, Jim Schott continues to live in the farmhouse on the property, and we meet him in his kitchen just a few paces from the farm's parking lot. A handsome man with wavy gray hair and bright blue eyes made more intense by his chambray work shirt, Jim speaks quietly in well-chosen words. Like us, he became interested in goats while leading a much different city life—he was a college professor and educational consultant—and he and his family bought property in Colorado with the intention of living closer to the land and raising a small herd of goats. Now, more than a decade later, Jim has expanded his operation, contracting with another local goat dairy for supplemental milk and building a new facility for the production of fresh cheeses (aged ones will continue to be made on the existing space). Through it all, Jim has insisted that the operation remain on a human scale and that it be available as a resource in the community.

Looking out on his property from the window near a towering wall of cookbooks, Jim echoes the sentiments we've heard from so many goat farmers: though he began his farm for personal reasons, the choices he's made have now assumed a greater weight. Near a large city, he considers his presence as a farmer imperative; a visit to his dairy may be the only experience that many locals—especially children—have with small-scale agriculture. Being able to see the goats and taste the cheeses that come from their milk makes a connection for visitors that Jim fears is all too rare.

On the day we visit, Haystack Mountain Dairy is open to the public. Everyone in Boulder seems to know about these weekly open houses, and as Jim shows us around the farm, there is a cheerful chaos of mothers and young children flitting between cheese samples, bottle feedings, and vigilant observation of the doe pen that has, earlier in the morning, produced a set of triplets. Spring is kidding season, and in almost every pen pregnant goats lie on distended bellies, moaning, puffy, and exhausted. When their kids finally emerge, they're quickly toweled off and taken to a separate barn where they're kept warm under heat lamps and bottle-fed with pasteurized colostrum.

In dairy herds this is not uncommon; the mother's milk is needed for cheese making so kids are taken to a separate "nursery" where they bond with the humans who feed them, making the goats more docile and people oriented as adults. Both the colostrum and the milk that they're subsequently fed are generally pasteurized to prevent the transmission of any pathogens that might be lurking.

This is sound disease prevention and is practiced by just about every commercial dairy in the country, but to many of the mothers who have brought their children to watch the goats, it's horrifying. Imagining giving birth and then having their babies taken away, some of them are indignant, demanding an explanation. Part of the education at Haystack Mountain Dairy is providing just that: demonstrating for visitors how dairies work, and how the cheese they enjoy would not be possible—or as healthy—without these practices. Nevertheless, the reactions to explanations from Amy, the herd manager, are mixed. "Maybe, but isn't there some other way?" a mother with her infant in a fleece baby sling asks plaintively. Amy, diplomatically, makes no comment when the same woman pulls out a plastic-wrapped package of string cheese for her older daughter (though we can imagine her thoughts: "If you think a small goat dairy's harsh, imagine a large commercial cow dairy.").

With all the visitors, sales of cheese are brisk. Farmworkers alternate between making change and ducking into the cheese cave, emerging with logs of fresh chèvre and aged Haystack Peak pyramids. On this blustery day, baskets of crackers are overturned on the outdoor tables and cheese samples include a few bits of grit, but visitors are undaunted. Everyone seems to be buying something.

Opening the dairy to the community is clearly a savvy business move, but more important, Jim has built in the opportunity to share his experiences and teach others about the realities of dairy farming. "No one farms for the money," he tells us, "it's the appeal of the lifestyle." It's an appreciation of the moments of calm while embracing those that are hectic. And above all, it's a love of the animals.

Exploring the pens with him, we see that Jim's affection for his goats is evident. Despite the dairy's expansion and the growing acclaim (in the coming years, Jim's cheeses, like Chef Folse's, will win awards from the American Cheese Society and will earn him mention among the top fifty cheese makers in the country in *Saveur* magazine), maintaining a relationship with the animals and an intimacy about the entire dairy is at the crux of Jim's approach. The farm is his business, but it is also his home in a large sense of the word. He sees the dairy—animals and employees—as a kind of family. Leaning in to nuzzle one of his bucks as though the massive goat were whispering in his ear, Jim looks completely connected with his world and perfectly content.

Heading over the Rockies and farther into the Southwest, Karl and I talk a lot about dairy goats and the trade-offs that come with them. In raising dairy animals, we would be forcing ourselves to confront all the emotional ambivalence that we've just skimmed in our travels. Not only would we have to separate newborn kids from their mothers—a practice I understand but still makes me ache—we would also have to decide which animals to cull from the herd.

In our visit with Jim, he told us a story about selling his extra spring kids to a man who wanted to roast one for Greek Easter. Arriving at the farm in a Mercedes and a tailored suit, the buyer opened his trunk, pulled out a pair of coveralls and a set of knives for butchering the carcass, and slaughtered and dressed the young goat on the spot. Without doing the slaughtering ourselves, or even being witness to it, by choosing the animals to cull, we would be responsible for their fate. It is a serious charge, and we simply aren't sure that we could do it. On the other hand, we're beginning to think that if we can't make those kinds of decisions, we have no business being carnivores, much less farmers.

For hundreds of miles—over craggy mountains, through deciduous forests, past dusty golden deserts—the conversations continue in our heads, erupting aloud at unexpected moments.

"I just don't think I can do it," I say suddenly, sitting bolt upright at three in the morning in our New Mexico campsite. Three hundred miles later, Karl blurts, "But if we're going to eat meat, then we have to accept the realities."

The reality is that in contemplating our fitness for farming, we're driving ourselves crazy.

Funnily enough, though we've expended a great deal of emotional energy on our choice of dairy goats, at this point in our travels we've never actually milked one. We've been to commercial dairies and small farms, we've tasted milk fresh from the udder, but as far as actually squeezing teats goes, we're complete novices.

At the Matrix Compound in Gallup, New Mexico, LaMancha owners Al Livingston and Bill Hanks change that. Just miles from the extensive Navajo reservation that borders Arizona, the land is barren and seems an unlikely place for an agricultural venture. Among the Navajo, however, raising goats and sheep is a way of life; Navajo women were traditionally given a small herd as a dowry, and recipes from the region are filled with mutton and goat meat, often used interchangeably. On our way to Bill and Al's, at The Eagle, a diner flanked by pawnshops (called, sadly, "trading posts") full of antique rugs, turquoise, and worked silver, Karl and I sample a traditional Navajo stew. Made with little more than meat and peppers and served with a side of hominy, the bowl is full of soft meat and brittle bones. Though on the menu it's called lamb stew, the shape of the bones makes us wonder if it might have been made with goat.

Outside town, Bill and Al live on a patch of desert that teems with life. Muscovy ducks greet us as we pull into the drive, a herd of LaManchas wanders its complex of pens, and in the house Al's young niece and nephew are visiting from the nearby reservation where they live. It's almost milking time when we arrive, and Al, shocked that we've never had a milking lesson, invites us into the barn, a small shed with walls covered with breeding charts and shelves holding hoof trimmers, collars, and grooming equipment.

The men mostly show their LaManchas—their first outing together in fact was to a goat show—and because they're not using the milk, they only milk the goats once a day. By evening, the goats' udders are full and swollen, practically dripping, ready to be drained. Usually they use a small pump, and while we talk they milk most of the does, leaving only two very docile animals.

A desert dusk has fallen outside, and the sky is a clear cobalt. In a pool of light from a single bulb in the barn's ceiling, Al's olive complexion deepens and his long black hair turns glossy. He leads a doe onto the milking stand, clipping her collar to the front. He invites me to sit on a low stool and shows me how to reach beneath the udder and grasp each teat.

"Form a ring with your fingers, and squeeze down," he instructs, gently stroking the doe's back to keep her calm.

I squeeze. Nothing comes out.

"Just keep closing your fingers around the teat, but relax. Give it a little tug down."

A tiny bead of milk gathers at the end of the teat. When I pull again, a weak dribble falls into the pail.

Al is phenomenally patient with us. He lightly massages the goat's udder, pulling gently at her teats to encourage her to let her milk down. He speaks softly to the doe, and each time he tugs, a stream of milk pours into the bucket. He asks if I want to try again. Enclosing my hands in his own, he demonstrates what my fingers are supposed to be doing.

This time, as I squeeze, a jet of milk misses the bucket and sprays my leg. The next time—I still can't figure out how—it runs up my wrist and into the arm of my sweatshirt. At one point, I shower Al's nephew, Cory, with a fine white mist. The barn is filled with a sweet, animal smell. Beneath my fingers the udder becomes rubbery; milk is emptying from it, though only about an inch ends up in the pail.

Karl learns a little from my mistakes, but his turn is similarly awkward. By the end, our hands ache and our backs hurt, our clothes are sticky and wet with milk. We are not naturals.

Far from dampening our enthusiasm for dairy goats, the experience actually fuels us. Despite our clear shortcomings, we're excited, as if we've aced some kind of test—this is what milking an animal feels like! We congratulate each other and talk excitedly about each detail, rehashing the experience: the intimacy we'd felt with the goat, the feeling of satisfaction as the emptying udder began to feel spongy and soft, the amazement that we'd been able to get any milk out at all.

"You were awesome!" I say to Karl.

"No, *you* were awesome!" he repeats.

Deep down, we know that neither of us was awesome, but we're still elated. My sweatshirt is covered in crusted milk (driving Godfrey crazy in the enclosed car) and our hands still feel the edge of a cramp as they curl around the steering wheel, but we feel, oddly enough, competent. We—Margaret Hathaway and Karl Schatz—have milked goats. It's hardly a shift in a milking parlor, but it's a start.

We pass through Phoenix while the Chicago Cubs are there for spring training. Through slightly devious means, we've arranged to go into the dugout and interview one of the players, backup middle infielder Ramón Martínez. A friend of Karl's who works at *Sports Illustrated* has told us that Martínez owns a restaurant in Puerto Rico, and we've pitched a story, never to be published, to a food magazine about sports figures who are foodies. In truth, this is just our cover. We want to ask an actual Cub about the Curse of the Billy Goat.

Once we're there, however, press passes clipped to our shirts, actually sitting in the dugout with Sammy Sosa and Dusty Baker (who notoriously despises all mention of the Curse), we're just too shy. We do a straight interview, jotting down notes about motivations and menu. The closest we get to goats is asking the player whether his restaurant serves cabrito. When he says yes, I shake my fist and whisper, "Eat the goat!" He laughs and claps me on the back.

Chapter 16

Our next destination is northern California, and after months on the road, approaching the vibrancy of a city like San Francisco is thrilling. We have crossed the entire country, driven from sea to shining sea. We have traversed windswept prairie, scaled rocky mountains, shaken red dust from our boots. We have slept in our car, in our tent, on people's sofas and lawns, have woken to dissipating mists, rosy dawns, and sharp farmhouse coffee. And now, tangled and dirty, we arrive in a town that's both elegant and cosmopolitan. In battered sneakers and unwashed clothes, we feel the contrast.

Karl and I both have close college friends who've settled in the Bay Area, and part of the treat of San Francisco is social. At this point in our journey we are changed; the last time we had seen our friends we were living in New York in what feels like a different lifetime. (In truth, this visit is a foretaste of what's to come in just a couple of months when we pass through New York on our way to Maine and wedding preparations.)

This is my first time in San Francisco, and we spend some of our stay—clean, well rested from sleeping in our friends' guest room—exploring the city. We marvel at the steep streets, forgetting which way to turn the wheels when we park on a hill and worrying that even in first gear, the Goat Mobile won't make it. We find our way to the City Lights bookstore, thumbing through volumes by the Beat poets. With my friend Katherine, we eat brioche and steaming café au lait at a French patisserie in the Mission District, while Godfrey sits at our feet at an outdoor table, sniffing passing city dogs and straining the leash to beg at our neighbor's table. On a clear day we take photos of the dog in front of the Golden Gate Bridge, white caps and Alcatraz obscured in the distance. And then, armed with the Chinese character for "goat" on a paper napkin we've carried since New York, we hit Chinatown.

In the time between beginning our Year of the Goat and finding ourselves in San Francisco's Chinatown, we've done a little research into the vagaries of Chinese goats. Mainland China, we've learned, is home to a variety of goat breeds, from the Guizhou white goat to the Jianchang black goat to the Qianbei pockmarked goat to the Nanjiang brown goat. While they are predominantly raised for cashmere and their fleece is exported, goat meat is widely consumed by the Chinese; given its population, the country is consequently the largest consumer of goat meat in the world.

In traditional recipes the goat is stewed. Contrary to many cultures that prize the meat of young spring kids and pair it with early spring vegetables, goats in China are generally eaten when they're older, and the meat is considered to be a winter food. Chinese goat consumption is said to rise substantially between October and February.

Unlike New York, San Francisco's Chinatown is not crowded claustrophobically with street vendors. Gradually the signs in the storefronts shift from English to Chinese, and the merchandise becomes thick with Hello Kitty. Cafés advertise bubble tea in their windows and bakeries display puffed dough rolled in sesame seeds and lotus seed cakes stamped with elaborate designs and varnished bright yellow with egg yolk. Starved for months of these treats, I buy a bag of pastries and a milky lavender mug of sweet taro root tea.

At every restaurant we pass, we poke our heads in and look at a menu, running our fingers down the edge of Chinese characters in search of *goat*. Meandering up and down the streets, we try all kinds: fancy restaurants, cafés festooned with paper lanterns, hole-in-the-wall lunch counters. Though we see lamb on the menu at one restaurant, the waiter assures us that they would never substitute goat.

Disappointed, we decide to try a grocery store. Passing through an entryway of dried seafood, mushrooms, and roots and a produce section of spiny melons and leathery red lychee nuts, we approach the meat counter. Poking our heads between a cluster of elderly women speaking voluble Chinese, we see, tucked between buckets of live frogs and trays of honeycomb tripe and chicken feet, a mound of shank bones marked with our symbol. We pull out our napkin and compare it with the sign; it looks the same. For confirmation, we ask a young woman who affirms with a wrinkle of her nose that we have found goat meat. We don't buy it, though we consider bringing it back as a present for our hosts, but we're glad to know it's there. We leave the shop triumphant.

The following day we are a world away at One Market Restaurant. Situated on an upscale corner near the Ferry Terminal Building, One Market is celebrated in the city, in part for the inventive menu of its chef, Adrian Hoffman. One of his projects, we've learned from the same food-writing friend who wrote out our Chinese character, is the introduction of goat meat to the gourmands of San Francisco. Every Thursday, he serves a goat meat special, sometimes roasted on a spit, but most often slow-cooked for up to eight hours.

Arriving at the restaurant in mid-afternoon when its tables are deserted and the kitchen is beginning to prepare for dinner, we're surprised by what we find. The restaurant is much more elegant than we'd anticipated. By Adrian's low-key demeanor when we'd set up the appointment, we'd expected something with the feel of a bistro, but instead are greeted with crisp, white linen; heavy, high-backed chairs; and abundant urns of flowers. Having come straight from an earlier visit at a farm just out of town, we're once again dusty and tracking bits of straw and goat droppings behind us. As is often the case when we meet members at the upscale end of the goat world, we are a little bedraggled and we know it. Embarrassed, we try to at least brush the goat hair off our pants before asking the maître d' to let Chef Hoffman know we've arrived for our appointment.

Adrian—a tall, lanky man in his thirties with short dark hair and glasses who has the air of an academic—comes out from the open kitchen and gallantly, given our disheveled appearance, sits with us at a table in the window to discuss his enthusiasm for goat. Compared to the goat meat advocates we've met across the country who are mostly farmers trying to develop a market for their livestock, Adrian's zest for goat seems at first improbable, but while talking with him we realize that's part of the appeal.

An avid traveler with a background in classical literature, Adrian first became interested in goat meat after tasting some traditional dishes in far-flung places around the Mediterranean. Associating goat's meat with the Classics—offerings to the gods, the desperate food of shipwrecked sailors, feasts for returning soldiers—he also liked the flavors of the meat, especially in combination with herbs, citrus, and olive oil. Later, when he had free rein to experiment at One Market, he decided to roast goat over an open flame in the restaurant's kitchen, which is visible to its patrons. He had a spit constructed and used it for other meats as well, but perhaps for its novelty, the goat caught people's attention. Restaurant goers began by ordering it for the swagger as much as the taste, but gradually the meat itself has developed a following.

What started as a foodie-style intellectual exercise has become something of an attraction.

As the months have passed, Adrian has shifted away from roasting the goat on a spit and has begun to cook it more slowly, braising it in a slow oven—not more than 250 degrees—for up to eight hours before serving. The resulting meat is meltingly tender, with an entirely different texture than he'd been able to achieve by spit roasting. Today the goat has been cooking since morning in a bath of olive oil, oregano, and lemon; for the dinner service, it will be pulled from the bone and shredded, then served in a mound with an egg and lemon sauce.

Throughout our conversation, Adrian's eyes have darted past us to the kitchen where he seems to be following the progress of dinner preparations. Standing from the table, he invites us to come back to the kitchen and have a look at the goat. The smell as he opens the oven door is unlike any we've associated with goat: pungent with herbs, sharp with citrus, with just a hint of the meat underneath. Adrian peels back the foil on one of the pans, and there's an intense release of steam. In the pan, the meat looks stewed and is dotted with defoliated branches of oregano and translucent slices of lemon.

As we marvel at the meat's aroma and texture, Adrian invites me—once I've washed up and put on some gloves—to help with the dinner preparations. For the next half hour, while Karl takes pictures, I dip my hands into the baking trays and pull hot meat from the bone, then shred it into another pan. The meat is scalding, and by the end of the tray my fingers are red and a little swollen, but the experience of readying goat meat to serve to San Francisco's upper crust is worth the pain.

A few hours later we return to One Market with some friends for dinner. After cocktails and appetizers, Karl and I order the goat with some braised broccoli rabe on the side; our friends are unconvinced.

Piled on our plates, the meat is drizzled with a foamy, pale yellow sauce. The goat is so tender it's nearly disintegrated—it barely needs to be chewed. Without the sauce, the meat is perfumed by the herbs and the oil. The flavor is so concentrated that each bite almost conjures a story: craggy mountains overlooking sparkling seas, capering goats, a lonely herder with a flute. Melting over the top, Adrian's egg and lemon sauce is rich and smooth, its flavors all yolk and fine zest. With the meat, the sauce brings out the flavor of the goat—its subtle hint of goatiness—while the lightness of its texture contrasts perfectly with the substantial meaty shreds. It is, by leaps and bounds, the best goat meat we taste in our travels.

As we're finishing coffees and profiteroles, something on the other side of the plate-glass window catches my eye. Surprisingly, it is Adrian Hoffman, astride a motorcycle, kicking the machine to life and roaring off into the late-spring evening. It seems an unlikely sight, but then so is his menu. That night the restaurant sells out of the goat special.

Chapter 17

W hile we're in San Francisco we feel a little self-conscious, contrasting our lives with those of our friends and feeling conspicuously goaty: the wacky, unemployed couple who drifts through town on part of a weird caprine quest. We've been on the road together for so long that we've become one of those couples who don't need to finish each other's sentences; we start our thoughts aloud and then drift off, confident that one knows where the other is headed. With old friends—friends who've known us before goats and even before we knew each other—we are suddenly aware of this habit. Even as we put on clean clothes and carry on a normal conversation about ideas, world events, and our shared histories, there's a part of us that feels like strange vagrants in the midst of our friends' lives of order and responsibility.

We know already that we have been changed by our pursuit, but we begin to wonder if we'll ever be able to return to lives of normalcy, or if now that we've found this passion for goats, we are both blessed by it and doomed forever to being oddballs. Can we be

farmers, back-to-the-landers, and maintain normal social lives? I
have visions of us in twenty years: me, looking crazed with stream-
ing white hair and dung-smeared coveralls; Karl, heavily bearded
but physically gaunt, with long, yellowed nails and bruised gouges
on the few fingers that still have their tips. I imagine the kind of attention we would attract at our college reunions, the embarrassment we would cause our children (or worse yet, what if they
weren't embarrassed?). We love goats, we want an agricultural life,
but this specter is grim.

Leaving San Francisco, we put these anxieties behind us. We're back
in traveling mode, trading our city black for frayed cargo pants and
hiking boots. I've put my hair in two braids under a bandanna; Karl's
beard, which seemed so big and bushy in San Francisco, feels once
more proportional. In rural northern California, we fit right in.

Across the Golden Gate Bridge, north of San Francisco in the
lush, rolling hills of Sonoma County where roads twist through manicured vineyards, we are on our way to visit Redwood Hill Farm, a
Grade A dairy that is the largest goat yogurt producer in the country,
before continuing up the coast to Eugene, Oregon, to visit my mom.

Based in Sebastopol, Redwood Hill Farm was founded on a much
smaller scale by the Bice family in 1968 and has been run since 1978
by the eldest daughter, Jennifer. As part of the early wave of women
cheese makers, Jennifer Bice is a friend of Capriole's Judy Schad and
a member of the loose sorority that vitalized the demand for goat's
milk products in the early eighties. She's also a savvy businesswoman:
her yogurt and cheeses are now sold throughout the United States,
and before we even considered embarking on our journey, I regularly
bought Redwood Hill's yogurt at Gourmet Garage in the West Village.

Though we're enthusiasts of the company's products, we've also
come to Redwood Hill to visit Steve Considine. An ADGA judge,
Saanen partisan, and lifetime dairy goat owner, Steve has worked at

Redwood Hill since 1981, and as the company has grown, his role has expanded to a sort of jack-of-all-trades. He is also a member of the Wisconsin Considine goat dynasty—son of Harvey and brother of the current ADGA president, Daniel Considine. While we're visiting the dairy, Steve has invited us to stay with him and has offered to show us his library of goat memorabilia, reputed to be one of the most interesting and extensive collections in the American dairy goat world.

On a bright spring day, we follow Steve's directions down increasingly smaller roads until suddenly the road ends in a livestock gate that spans a winding dirt drive. Beyond it, we see not goats but sheep and assorted poultry wandering among lush gardens. We open the gate and drive in, not certain that we've come to the right place, and even less so when we find a thin man in tailored shorts and an oxford cloth shirt squatting with a trowel among ripening melons, greens, and thick-stalked, nearly blooming artichokes.

The man is Steve's landlord, in whose weekend home he rents an apartment. Part of the rent is bartered; during the week, Steve acts as caretaker for the property's sheep, chickens, ducks, geese, and dogs. Steve's goats, it turns out, are integrated into the Redwood Hill herd.

Though he isn't yet home, Steve has left word that we're to make ourselves comfortable. The apartment is open, with two bedrooms and a patio extending behind it into terraced gardens. The walls are lined with bookshelves holding dozens of books on goats but also works of fiction and on travel. Several guidebooks to England are scattered on a table, and we learn later that Steve is about to leave on a vacation to visit some British friends, take in the Royal Horticultural Society's Chelsea Flower Show, a handful of goat shows, and see the birthplace of James Herriot, country veterinarian and author of *All Creatures Great and Small*. Steve collects satyrs, and on the shelves and walls are mugs, figurines, and posters of Puck. When his truck pulls in, the vanity plate reads SATYR. We can't help looking around, but inside the apartment we feel uncomfortably like we're snooping, so we sit in the back reading and admiring the plants until Steve arrives.

Steve Considine is a jolly-looking man with a round belly, rosy cheeks, and a full white beard. Wearing denim overalls in his garden, he reminds me of a gnome. Raised in Portage, Wisconsin, he has lived in California since the 1970s. For a time before moving west, he worked for a veterinarian in Lancaster County, Pennsylvania, treating the animals of the Amish, whom Steve admires and whose practices he considers a model for land stewardship. But in Sonoma County he found community, satisfying work, and beautiful land, marred only, he says, by gophers, "the scourge of northern California." Here, he lives a quiet life, knitting, gardening, baking bread, and caring for his nine Saanen does. Though he enjoys traveling, northern California is his sanctuary.

While we're sitting on the patio talking, Steve serves some cheeses he's brought home for us to sample. On a cheese board, he puts out a small, earthy button of Redwood Hill California Crottin, still a bit crumbly, though lightly aged, with a soft white rind. Next to it he unwraps a round of Camellia, a sweet goat's milk Camembert with a center so ripe it runs out like thick cream. The Bucheret, Redwood Hill's variant of the French *bûcheron*, is pungent, ripened with a light rind on the outside but still dense in the center, with a flavor that's faintly herbed. Nibbling on cheese and homemade bread in Steve's garden, we can see why he stayed: his is an earthly paradise.

After dinner, Steve brings out his collection of goat memorabilia. It is truly an archive, boxes of antique dairy goat journals, copies of books on goats in French and Italian, correspondence relating to the sale of prominent animals. When the poet Carl Sandburg's wife, Paula, sold her herd of prize-winning Saanens, the Considine family bought a substantial number, and notes about that sale are included among the papers. There are turn of the century magazines extolling the virtues of goat's milk and ads for champion bucks written in the same vaguely huckstering language as those found in the back of goat publications today. In one book, Steve shows us a photo illustration of a nurse suckling a human baby directly on a goat's teat: the infant lies on its back in a woven basket wearing a lacy white gown, its body fitting neatly between the goat's front and back legs.

Before bed, Steve gives us a copy of *La Chèvre*, a French goat treatise by Joseph Crepin originally published in 1906 and reprinted in 1990 with an introduction and extensive commentary by Steve. A compendium of goat facts, photographs, and history, *La Chèvre* is an artifact of another age, but it also shows, almost eerily, how some aspects of the goat world haven't changed. Within the text, black-and-white photos depict goat owners squinting out toward the camera, wearing variations on the dirndl and lederhosen, peaked Tyrolean hats, capes, and many-buttoned vests. In each photo, the goats are posed in exactly the same stance they're judged in at contemporary goat shows.

In the morning, we go to Redwood Hill. At the time of our visit, Redwood Hill Farm feels like two very distinct businesses: one raises goats and makes cheese in a cluster of barns and pale, stuccoed buildings that overlook miles of vineyards; the other holds nondescript office space and a yogurt production facility set behind chain-linked fences among warehouses on a block of asphalt. Until earlier this year, Redwood Hill's yogurt had been made, packaged, and distributed by another company that followed Redwood Hill's recipes and specifications but took care of logistics. A few months ago, however, that company was bought by a larger producer and Redwood Hill in turn bought the yogurt-making equipment. When we visit, Redwood Hill is in the process of becoming entirely self-sufficient, having just increased its full-time staff and begun production. The company's plan is to integrate the two parts of the business, housing everything—offices, cheese making, and yogurt production—under one roof, but for now everything is miles apart.

Our first stop is at the production facility where the bustle of activity animates every corner. Though the company employs only about twenty people, on the production floor the scale is staggering: yogurt cultures ripen in immense vats, a mechanized filling machine squirts the cultured milk into cups, conveyor belts move everything along. All of the machinery is shiny and much of it is loud; the air smells of both a tangy hint of goat's milk and a humid wash of bleach. The space is immense and except for the production line, much of it is empty. Looking around the high ceilings and cavernous rooms, the building strikes me as something to be measured in volume. Behind heavily insulated doors, one balmy room incubates the yogurt at 110 degrees, while another stores it at a chilly 34. In each, pallets holding flats of yogurt are stacked to the top of thirty-foot ceilings.

There are no animals here, except for the smiling, lavender beribboned goat wreathed in laurels that adorns every yogurt cup. The milk is brought in by truck, and while the whiz of mechanization makes this a fascinating place to visit, we wonder if the line of workers in hairnets and lab coats, to whom we overhear Steve speaking in fluent Spanish, have any interest in goats.

At the farm and cheese plant a couple miles away, the environment is completely different. There the goats live in a series of barns that fan out from a central cheese-making building. When we arrive, following Steve's truck through a maze of rural roads, the cheese makers are eating lunch at an outdoor table on a flagstone veranda that overlooks the verdant hills of a neighboring winery. The group, a mixture of students from a nearby agricultural college and interns from France and Bulgaria, sprawl loosely as they share salads, bread, and cheese. They milk the goats twice daily and make cheese six days a week, yet no one looks exhausted or worn out or tired of the goats; in fact, they all seem relaxed and a little exhilarated.

In the barns, where Alpines, Saanens, and a few LaManchas and Nubians are kept, we stop with Steve to visit his Saanens, who nuzzle him affectionately. He points out little delicate polka dots on their noses, ears, and udders. Saanens are pure white, and rather than tanning, their skin freckles. Scratching their necks and shoulders, Steve leans down to the does and says quietly, "If you're sweet, beautiful, and healthy, you can stay in this barn."

The goats are among the most attractive we've seen: tall, well-formed animals, exemplifying breed standards, without a trace of illness. This shouldn't surprise us, given that both Steve and the Bice family have been active in the world of show goats, but the accumulation of so many handsome animals is a sight to behold. We know that it's taken decades to build the herd, and the animals look this good because they are so well cared for. They are happy goats, and their rich milk produces wonderful cheese. It sounds a little corny, but standing among them, the Redwood Hill goats are an inspiration. These are the kind of animals we want.

We pack a cooler with some goat yogurt and cheese to give my mother, and then we leave Redwood Hill Farm to head farther north, following Route 101. Though the drive is foggy, we stop several times to look out at the ocean, the color of slate on this overcast day. At one point, we pull off for lunch in a small town and take a path down rickety wooden steps to walk Godfrey on the beach. He splashes in the surf, then chews on ropes of rubbery kelp. We're not sure why it hits us now, but watching the dog play in the Pacific, we're struck by the idea that we've crossed the entire country.

It feels, somehow, like a monumental point in our journey. We've reached the far shore, touched the other ocean. In the nine months since we left New York, we've explored myriad paths, both within ourselves and without. We've had all kinds of adventures, and at the same time our barely formed goat dreams have coalesced into something concrete, taking us in a single direction where we've found models and mentors to emulate. Visiting the Boltons and then the

Boehles, we've experienced a way of living as a family that resonates with us. From Judy Schad and Jim Schott we've realized the true necessity of becoming a small farmer, environmentally, socially, and politically. From so many, we've tasted flavors, both in cheeses and meats, that have inspired and humbled us. We know that our next great journey—creating worthy cheeses of our own—will be epic.

Standing on the beach, we collect little pieces of driftwood rounded by the waves. Sandy and salty, we feel as though we've accomplished something just by getting here, but we know that there are still many miles to go.

Chapter 18

From California we travel north to Eugene, Oregon, where we spend a few days visiting my mom on her sabbatical. There we explore the vast farmers' market, where my mother has enthusiastically told us she's been introduced to obscure varieties of kale, subtle local honeys, and numerous craftspeople. While she would never dream of pressuring us, as we walk through the stalls she lingers at a booth of organic cotton baby clothes.

In the studio apartment she's been renting, we share the cheeses we've brought her—her eyes close and she gets a blissed-out smile at her first bite of the Camellia—then go walking in a hazelnut grove down the street. The fruit is green, but from a bordering alley berry canes droop heavily with raspberries and deep purple blackberries. We marvel at this fertility; Karl and I walk along the street browsing like goats.

A few days later, north of Spokane, Washington, outside the little town of Rice in the Pleasant Valley, we stop at the farm of Rick and

Lora Lea Misterly, owners of Quillisascut Cheese Company. Although we don't know it when we arrive, theirs is our fantasy life. We will leave Quillisascut knowing exactly what—and who—we want to become.

Situated at the top of a hill in the middle of the Misterlys' thirty-six and a half acres, the buildings of Quillisascut Cheese Company are modest, and because they are somewhat recessed into the ground, give the illusion of being much smaller than they are. Rick, a wiry man dwarfed by blue coveralls and a hooded sweatshirt, and his wife, Lora Lea, equally active but with a calmer energy and a soft, kind face, have lived on the property since 1981. They bought the place with the goal of self-sufficiency and have gradually achieved it, paying off their initial mortgage and refusing to take on any debt for expansion. Over the years, they've built their home, cheese rooms, barns, and a retreat house, pacing construction and trading favors with handy friends so that they never have to borrow money. They've been making cheese for seventeen years, and since 1989, when Rick quit working off the farm as a carpenter, their land has provided their sole income.

"Anyone who gets into farming to make a huge profit is crazy," says Rick emphatically, echoing a joke we heard from Judy Schad: How do you make a small fortune in goats? Start with a large one. But the Misterlys have found a quality and rhythm of life that suits them. They are not wealthy, but they have enough.

In the time that they've been making cheese, Rick and Lora Lea have been part of Seattle's cheese market as its appetite has expanded from limited to voracious. Though seasonally they make other types of cheeses, throughout the year the Misterlys' cheese of choice is a raw goat's milk *manchego*, a firm Spanish cheese made traditionally with whole sheep's milk. Manchego can be eaten at one of three stages of ripening: *fresco* (fresh), *curado* (aged between three and four months), or *viejo* (aged even longer). The texture is semihard, similar to Swiss cheese (but without the holes), and the cheese is often grated for cooking. The Misterlys slightly age their cheese; it's ready when it's curado. They also add sweet lavender and fennel or piquant ground chilies to the cheese, selling it in creamy white wheels dotted with flecks of spice and marked with black-and-white stickers that read: "Gourmet Cheese from the Pampered Pets of Pleasant Valley." Annually they sell more than five thousand pounds to Seattle's restaurants, cheese shops, and grocers.

The milk for this cheese comes entirely from their small herd of goats, which ranges from thirty-five to forty milking does a season. They choose not to keep purebred animals but instead breed each year for traits they'd like to improve. To increase the butterfat, one year they bred their Alpines and Saanens to a Nubian buck, as the milk from Nubians has consistently high-fat solids. (In much of the dairy goat world, this kind of miscegenation is unheard of and would even seem shocking.)

Their milking technique is equally unorthodox. Twice daily, Rick and Lora Lea milk their does by hand, leading them five at a time onto a waist-high ledge Rick built around the perimeter of the milking parlor. The ledge is high enough to allow Rick and Lora Lea to stand while milking. They squeeze the goats' teats into milk pails, then empty them through a filter into milk canisters that Lora Lea hauls down to her cheese room. Rather than using inflation pumps and glass tubing, the Misterlys do things the old-fashioned way, with their hands and a bucket. We timidly ask if we can help in the morning. When they agree, I become suddenly nervous, hoping that Karl and I have magically become more competent in the drive from New Mexico.

Though this part of Washington becomes parched by summer—it receives only twelve inches of rain annually—in the late spring when we're visiting Pleasant Valley is a lush, hazy green. For the rest of the afternoon, Rick shows us around his gardens, taking us through the goat pen and up a hill to rows of vegetables, almond and walnut trees, and orchards of fruit. Lower on the land, outside Lora Lea's cheese room, he's experimenting with wine grapes, and small green clusters hang from vines he identifies as Syrah, cabernet franc, pinot noir, and gewürztraminer. Muscovy ducks, Bourbon Red toms, and various breeds of chickens wander about the property. In a lower pasture, Rick points out a few grazing cows.

Periodically as we're walking around, Karl catches my eye or squeezes my hand. The Misterlys' farm fairly sings to us with a siren's call of all we hope for ourselves. As Rick tells us more about their operation—the summer culinary retreats they run for Seattle's food professionals, the straw bale building methods they've used on the retreat house, the local Slow Food Upper Columbia convivium, the disks of seasonal *marc de raisin* cheese they pack in pressed grape skins—we find ourselves imagining their lives as our future.

The simplicity with which they live is breathtaking, and we marvel especially at how little they waste. Whey from the cheese is composted or given to a neighbor's piglets, animal manure is returned to the garden.

Lora Lea recounts her horror last summer when some of the culinary students on retreat used an entire bag of lemons to make lemonade and then discarded the peels. She takes us into a pantry in the retreat house and shows us a sign that prohibits throwing away citrus rinds. Underneath it are rows of Ball jars filled with preserves. She laughs about her reaction at the time (she gave the students a long, guilt-inspiring lecture, "just like I was their mother"), but her tone is matter of fact when she says, "It was just so wasteful. You know, citrus doesn't grow here, so it's a luxury. Now, if students want to use the juice, they also have to make marmalade, or candied peel, or pickled lemon rinds."

The idea for the retreats originated as a way of putting food into context, and they began two years earlier with an invitation to the chefs who buy Quillisascut cheese to visit the farm. Gradually, the retreats have evolved into internships. Now a series of sessions, funded in part by the tail end of a university grant from the Kellogg Foundation, can accommodate up to ninety-six students per summer. During week-long sessions, the culinary professionals who attend—from chefs to natural foods store owners to food writers to hospital kitchen staff—take part in milking goats, making cheese, butchering animals, and gathering their own ingredients from the garden. Each day begins with a word, starting on the first day with "respect," and moving on to others like "community" and "sustainability." Rick and Lora Lea now see these sessions as catalysts for reconnection with the origins of one's food.

"Even people who've been in the kitchen for decades may not have ever seen an animal being slaughtered," explains Rick, telling us about the lesson in which they butcher a sheep. The students may find it disturbing (most do), and may never witness another slaughter, but his point is to show them exactly where meat comes from before it's packed in a truck and delivered to their restaurants.

We've arrived at the farm late in the day, and the air chills as the sun dips behind a jagged ridge of distant conifers. The four of us stay up talking and drinking wine far later than is reasonable, given the hour that we need to milk the goats. When Karl and I tumble into twin beds in the retreat house, it's past midnight, but we lie in the dark, energized, nervous about the milking, talking about the future.

At five, we straggle into the thin light to find Rick and Lora Lea already in the milking parlor. The room has really been built for two milkers, and we feel awkward and out of place hovering around, offering to carry or move whatever we can to help. There is a sort of drawbridge to the ledge on which the goats are milked, and Rick lowers and secures it as Lora Lea fills the grain buckets at each stanchion with barley. The goats come in five at a time, and in each group, Rick and Lora Lea greet them and choose which animals Karl and I will milk. We are given the easiest does, the ones that have sweet temperaments, smaller udders, larger teats, and no trouble letting down their milk. The room is quiet, except for the crunch of goats chewing and the sharp metallic sound of a milk stream hitting the side of the pail at regular intervals. Though our presence disrupts their routine, the Misterlys are quickly in the rhythm of milking—Rick has described it as a meditative state.

Milking a goat while standing is completely unlike our previous, seated, milking experience. There is considerably less torquing of our bodies, and the goats' udders are almost at eye level. We're hesitant, and our first squeezes are tentative, producing just trickles of milk as we stand far back from the animals and their unpredictable hooves. We come closer as we become more comfortable, finally leaning our cheeks against the goats' bellies as we ease into a hypnotic rhythm. It takes us a very long time and our hands are cold and cramped before we're through, but the animal warmth of goats in the morning starts our day gently. It's as though we are truly waking up as we milk.

As each bucket is filled, Lora Lea pours it through a filter and into a large jug, then dumps off the creamy foam for the barn cats that immerse themselves in it as if in a waterfall, white froth clinging to their furry ears. They mewl and lap up the cream, and we see another instance of integration: nothing is wasted.

We leave Quillisascut with a new understanding of what we want to do, and who we want to be. Rick and Lora Lea's parting advice to us is if we want to farm, we should just do it. No amount of planning or research will truly prepare us—we just need to go out and do. We realize, cutting the corners across Montana, Idaho, and down into Wyoming, that they're right.

In their final words, Rick and Lora Lea have delivered a kind of keynote address, charging us with a new mission to go forward into the agricultural life. It feels, in a sense, like our quest is over: we've hunted for nine months, and now we've found the treasure. We want to farm, we have a model for the kind of life we want to create, and now it's all up to us.

Chapter 19

After the epiphanies of Quillisascut, we consider calling our project complete. We've asked the tough questions, and armed with their answers we feel like we're ready for the next step. We know exactly what we want to do—though we may bicker over details, we agree that never in our adult lives have we had such clarity of purpose and such sure direction. Before we start the rest of our lives, however, we've committed to one final western stop.

The main street of Lander, Wyoming, is suffused with golden light as we drive into town on a chilly May evening. Nestled in the foothills of the Wind River Mountains, Lander's population is small but includes a disproportionately large community of environmentalists, outdoors folk, and ranchers. It is a base for watchdog groups, an outpost of the National Outdoor Leadership School (NOLS), which is akin to Outward Bound, and home to Wind River Pack Goats. It's this last that has brought us to Lander: we're going goat packing.

We'd heard about pack goats, and specifically those trained by John Mionczynski, since the ADGA convention we attended in October. John is widely regarded as the father of American goat packing and has at times also been an active member of ADGA; a talented musician, we'd heard stories from people as disparate as Judy Schad and Marge Kitchen about him entertaining ADGA conventioneers with impromptu sessions of jazz piano.

A biologist by training, John began taking pack goats out with him on extended studies of bighorn sheep that he conducted for the National Park Service. Their efficiency and companionship struck him: as pack animals, goats are both exceptionally agile and light on the environment, nibbling their way along the narrowest of trails while leaving little effect on the local ecosystems. Especially in dry land, goats' minimal impact on the biological soil crust—the thin microbial layer that covers arid earth—makes them perfect for packing. Carrying up to one-third of their body weight, browsing on scrub along the trail, goats enable a hiker to go out for days with little more than a light rucksack.

As so many others we'd encountered, John's involvement in the world of goats deepened gradually, from an interest to a livelihood. In 1987, he founded Wind River Pack Goats, becoming an outfitter and guide as well as a builder of custom goat saddles. In 1992 he published *The Pack Goat*, a practical instruction book about the care and training of pack goats, which is also a really fun read.

John is something of a legend among those who dabble in goat packing. Before coming to Lander, he was mentioned to us by everyone who had even a vague interest in goat packing. Like many acclaimed animal trainers, his name (which few people can pronounce with confidence) is spoken with reverence and a little awe, as though he has some mysterious, deep connection with his goats. His stories—soothing his animals with accordion tunes, reprimanding them with a short puff of cigar smoke, trusting them when their body language tells him to turn back—are the stuff of fiction, though when he explains each circumstance to us, these methods seem totally reasonable. After going on one trip with him, we find that even seasoned goat packers defer to us as if by being in John's presence we've somehow absorbed wisdom at the feet of the master. At a goat packing workshop the following year, even, we're treated like experts and asked to saddle a goat for demonstration— something we do slowly and very inexpertly.

We are, in fact, lucky to be going out with John at all. Several years earlier, he sold the business to Charlie Wilson and now only occasionally comes along on trips. He continues to own goats, pack animals that are integrated with the Wind River herd and a few dairy goats that he keeps at Twin Creek Ranch outside Lander, but for the most part he now devotes his time to biological research. On this trip, however, John is coming along to give us a tutorial on edible plants; packing with a milking doe, he says, you can bring absolutely nothing and continue to eat well.

We arrive in Lander the day before our trip is scheduled to begin. Having e-mailed sporadically with Charlie beforehand, we've arranged to spend the night camping in his backyard after boarding Godfrey at a local vet. We find his house easily; a burgundy van painted with Wind River's logo is parked out front.

Before buying Wind River Pack Goats, Charlie spent a decade working for NOLS, leading semester-long trips in Africa and shorter adventures in the American West. Meeting us at his front door, flanked by his yellow Labs, Gordon and Calypso, Charlie is the trip leader every college girl spending her junior year in Kenya has a crush on: tall, with dark hair and blue eyes, a Brahmin pedigree, and a laid-back but quietly authoritative manner. Originally from Providence, Rhode Island, his family was in the newspaper business, and he's known enough material comfort to pursue a different path. He has worked as a high school science teacher and a family therapist, and his demeanor immediately inspires confidence and trust. In just a few minutes, we are totally convinced of his competence and, strangely, have affirmed our own.

During this last leg of our journey west, things had become a little tense. We knew now that we wanted our future to be on a farm, but before we could settle we had to get through the summer and the wedding. The ceremony seemed to be approaching at breakneck speed, and while we had no doubt that we were committed to each other, a few moments had flared into argument and, for me, raging hives. After leaving Quillisascut, on a winding road in Washington a disagreement about our wedding registry—I still voted for kitchen appliances, Karl wanted farm equipment—had left my torso covered in raised red welts. As if a big fight in a small car in the middle of nowhere weren't awful enough, I was swollen and scratching, and scarily visible at the collar of my shirt, my trunk was scarlet. No amount of Benadryl or Calamine lotion would relieve the hives, nor would the make-up blackberry milkshake Karl bought me from a modified train car in downtown Spokane. As excited as we'd been anticipating the goat packing trip, at this point, after five weeks on the road, I am tired, stressed, and above all, itchy.

And then we meet Charlie, whom I immediately trust enough to confide in. He's going out for the evening but recommends that I use his tub to take an oatmeal bath, laying out soft, clean towels before he leaves. I soak, then Karl and I go to dinner at Cowfish, a restaurant in downtown Lander recommended by Charlie that uses local ingredients in its kitchen and makes its own beer. After a good meal, we pitch our tent under cold, starry skies, and relaxed by the bath and ready for the next day's adventure, the world feels better.

By morning there's frost on the tent, and we awaken, snuggled together through our sleeping bags, to the snuffles of Gordon and

Calypso who've come over to investigate. From the pale light, almost watery through the fabric of our tent, we can tell that it's early, but we hear voices outside and emerge to find that other goat packers have begun to arrive.

In all there will be seven of us hiking with the goats: Charlie, John, the two of us, and three strangers. The two who have just arrived are Tom and Elizabeth, a father and daughter who have met up in Wyoming for a goat adventure. Tom, a former Marine, seems skeptical about the goats—and even more so about us, as we straggle out of Charlie's backyard in our pajamas—but Elizabeth is enthusiastic and is thinking of training a goat of her own at home in Florida. The third to arrive is Beverly, a fit Forest Service worker from Colorado, who is also interested in getting goats of her own.

John arrives shortly after, a lean, weathered man with short brown hair, a mustache, and improbably white teeth. He clearly travels light, and everything about him seems somehow unencumbered: his carriage is erect but relaxed, he brings just one rucksack, his cargo pants seem to hold nothing but a pocketknife. He doesn't speak much, letting Charlie lead us through the introductions and waivers. I'm wearing a fund-raising shirt from KMUW, Wichita's public radio station, that reads, "Lend an ear to public radio," beneath a self-portrait of Vincent Van Gogh (the back reads, groaningly, "Gogh 89.1 FM!"). At one point, when I've unzipped my jacket, John comes over to silently scrutinize my T-shirt, then simply nods his head.

We gather our things and, as a group, learn how to distribute weight in the panniers and load them onto the saddles, which for now are balanced on saw horses. Piled into the van, we drive outside town to collect the goats, which live on a patch of land bordering the large swath of Bureau of Land Management hills where we'll be hiking. The goats are confined to several fenced acres: red hills covered in sagebrush, ravines they can scramble through, shaded structures for resting around a close courtyard of feeders.

Because we are novices and this is an introductory trip, Charlie has chosen the most docile goats, but as we round them up—luring them with alfalfa treats, being careful not to touch their horns, tentatively clipping on their leads—I find myself inexplicably drawn to another. He is a brown goat with one broken horn and a tremendous overbite, and he's clearly picked on by the other goats. I imagine him bullied on the playground, wearing glasses. His name is Panzer, and by Charlie's and John's accounts, he is the worst of the pack goats— dreamy, spacey, continually wandering off, or being left behind. Panzer will not be coming with us, but after just this one encounter, I harbor a secret crush on him.

Our trip is three days long, and throughout it we spend the days in easy hikes, break early to set up camp, and in the evenings learn more specifics about goat care. By day, we carry nothing more than a light pack, filled with just a water bottle, journal, and maybe a camera (or, in Karl's case, half a dozen, with various lenses). Setting up camp, we round up the goats and collect our tents, sleeping bags, and heavier packs of clothes and toiletries. During our lessons in goat care, John and Charlie instruct us as we saddle and unsaddle the goats, drawing straps tightly across their diaphragms and loosely looping another beneath the tail.

"You'll want to check the saddle pad for burrs—they can cause some nasty irritations," Charlie reminds us as we pair up and choose practice goats.

"Make sure you can fit two fingers between the goat and the cinch," John says, demonstrating how to tighten the buckles behind the goats' front legs.

On the second evening, we get a lesson in hoof trimming, using orange-handled clippers that look much like gardening shears. I enthusiastically volunteer to help, taking John's instructions to follow the length of the hoof, clipping the sides until they're almost even with the center's spongy frog. I snub the front point just a bit, then, feeling a little proud of myself, move on to the next hoof. It's hubris that gets me. I finish the back hooves, but on the front, the goat flinches while I'm snipping and I nearly prune off the tip of my finger. I don't even shout, just gasp, when blood begins to drip from the deep cut I've made in my finger. I'm intent on finishing the trimming, but by the end I'm leaving bloody fingerprints on the last hoof. Before dinner, Charlie bandages me up, and the goats are untethered for the evening, belled but free to roam.

Meals are much more lavish than we'd expected. Charlie has loaded the goats with an immense camp stove, and on it he makes things like fajitas, and in the morning, fried eggs and hash browns. Throughout the day during our walks, John points out edible plants, picking flowers and shoots from the crumbled dirt of the trail and offering them to whoever is closest.

"This one's got a pretty strong onion flavor," he'll say, handing back a cluster of purple buds. "This one's got a little bite." One plant will clot blood (I could have used it after the hoof trimming, I joke), and he tells a story of packing it into a wound on the trail. Another is an astringent. A third is a natural deworming agent for goats; it's extremely bitter, but they love it.

In truth, we've begun the trip a little intimidated by John, both because of his reputation and his self-containment. But then one evening, sitting in our campsite cradled by an amphitheater of red rock, John unzips his canvas bag. From it he pulls an antique wooden squeeze-box, and as the sky turns a deep azure, he begins to play, first a polka then a maudlin Scottish tune.

We had wrongly assumed from his knowledge and comfort on the trail that John was a Wyoming native. In fact, he grew up in a Polish family in the suburbs of New York City. His interest was always in biology and the outdoors—as a child, he performed experiments breeding praying mantises in his family's basement—and while attending

Long Island University, he was drawn west, first on trips with a friend and then for good. In the course of his research, he has narrowly escaped being crushed by an avalanche, has been struck twice by lightning, and has gone out for months at a time with nothing but his equipment and his goats. His home outside Lander is a little cabin, barely accessible by vehicle, that is electrified by a car battery.

John's is a respect we feel is worth earning, and this, as much as anything else, keeps us focused on the trip. Rather than making mental lists of all the wedding tasks that still need to be accomplished, or scratching the hive blotches that are now confined to the line of my waistband and the straps of my daypack, I taste the plants, trim the hooves, and concentrate on the sky. Though there are a dozen goats with us, I learn their names, calling out to Frosty, Moe, and Zuko when they stray from the path and scratching their warm, bristled backs when they come close. The expanse of hills, unmarred by power lines, is breathtaking; above us, great cumulous clouds hover as if flattened on sheets of glass. It's impossible not to surrender to the setting, to give myself over to the gamey whiffs of goat and dusty sagebrush, to the vivid, almost dizzying colors of the trail. Without a heavy pack to carry, it's like taking a long, head-clearing stroll.

At lunch on our last day out, eating chocolate pudding that Charlie has garnished with Scharffen Berger chocolates I've donated from the half pound my mother slipped into the Goat Mobile's glove box, I'm not ready for the trip to be over. I feed apple cores to the goats, lazily scratching their foreheads, and feel almost a sadness about returning to our real lives. If we could, I think we would stay out here forever. As it is, after lunch we begin our descent from the hills, stepping aside for the goats to lead as we make our way single file down the thin thread of a ledge.

The following week Charlie is leading a trip to the Red Desert. As we repack our car in his driveway, telling him what a wonderful time we've had, he asks us if we'd like to come along on this next adventure. The trip is small, he says, and he'd like to add more personalities to the mix; rather than paying for the trip, he offers to barter for some of Karl's photos.

We can't decide on the spot—back in civilization, we're once more governed by our real-life concerns and timetable—and we're quietly debating, when he utters the fateful, magical words: "We can bring Panzer."

The Red Desert is an arid basin the size of Connecticut, formed by a split in the Continental Divide. Its landscape is nearly lunar: white, cracked flats over powdery soil, weathered sandstone formations in striated reds, yellowed ridges and peaks dulled by millennia of wind. Because of its elevation—an average of sixty-eight hundred feet—the desert is home to no snakes, a source of great relief after the warnings we'd received about rattlesnakes in the brush of the Wind River foothills. What does inhabit the Red Desert, we'd see with amazement and hear one night thundering through our camp, are herds of wild horses.

This journey inspires in us the same feelings of wonder and solace as the previous, but on this trip we drift a bit more in our heads. The group, both of people and of goats, contains all levels of skill, and we string ourselves along, visible at any distance in the desert. One afternoon the sweeping purple of the sky announces an approaching storm, then splits with a crack of lightning; one morning we awaken to find a dusting of snow on the ground and a goat nuzzling against us through the fabric of our tent. A lone horse follows us at a great distance, returning every so often to his herd; we call him their scout.

Panzer is, to put it kindly, not naturally gifted as a pack goat. Each day Charlie gives me a handful of alfalfa treats to lure Panzer along the trail. The other goats trek up narrow ledges, panniers scraping the rock, pebbles breaking free and raining down the sides. Panzer surveys the scene and waits. Coaxing him when he's distracted, cajoling him when he's stopped, I compose haiku to Panzer in my head:

Beaked more than toothy
Browsing is tricky for me
Ah, tender young shoots.

The atmosphere on this trip is more convivial this time than educational. In the evenings we share bottles of wine and single-malt whiskey. Charlie smokes a cigar after dinner and tells us about his collection of antique Oliver tractors and BMW motorcycles, about the time he tried, disastrously, to teach his dog Gordon to ride in the sidecar. In the mornings we awake to elaborate pancake breakfasts; in addition to twenty gallons of water, the goats have packed in a griddle.

When we return to Lander we meet up again with John Mionczynski who has promised to introduce us to his dairy goats. Boarded at Twin Creek Ranch, a holistic cattle ranch and bed-and-breakfast owned by pioneering ranchers and environmentalists Tony and Andrea Malmberg, these goats live with a small herd that Andrea may eventually milk for cheese.

The Malmbergs focus on grass-fed beef, raised under environmentally sound conditions, but they are no strangers to goats. Tony's sister, Lani, owns twelve hundred cashmere goats that she travels with and rents out for weed management (and that have actually cleared much of the Twin Creek property). Their own herd of dairy goats, however, is housed far from the rest of their ranch. In an old, wooden barn, near the crumbling stone foundation of an early homestead, we meet John's goats. Above us a wood rat clings to a rafter, her babies latched on and swinging precariously from her teats. John, tenderly scratching his doe, reaches for her full udder, and bending to the ground, squirts warm milk into his open mouth and my cupped hands. We are all a long way from New York.

Several months later, when Karl and I have married, Charlie gives us Panzer as a wedding present. The goat, he says flatteringly, blossomed under my attention, and he thinks he would be happier away from the Wind River herd. At the time, we are living in an apartment in downtown Portland, Maine, and although we're looking for property in the country, we're a little unsure of what to do with the goat without land on which to keep him. But we have such affection for him that we'll go to any lengths. We talk with several area farms about boarding him and are in the process of arranging a rendezvous to collect him in, of all places, Chicago, when Panzer gets a horn infection that spreads to his brain. Charlie keeps us posted, as for several days Panzer's behavior is erratic. Then one morning, just before Thanksgiving, Charlie finds his body.

Karl and I are both heartbroken, and a little relieved. Charlie is a seasoned goatherd, stoic about the loss of animals. He carries a gun on the trail, and he tells us that he has used it to put down even his favorite goats when illness or injury struck. We're new to this, though, and if our beloved Panzer had died in our care, it would have been shattering. As much as we wanted to give him a happier, more comfortable life, we console ourselves; if Panzer was so ill, his death may have been for the best. A few weeks later, in time for the holidays, we receive a box from Charlie; it contains Panzer's horn.

Chapter 20

We return to New York at the end of June. The car is packed with a year's worth of goat detritus: brochures for fencing, back issues of the *Dairy Goat Journal*, boxes stuffed with Year of the Goat T-shirts, and puppet-making supplies. A dozen more boxes, packed with early wedding presents, extra clothing, and more goat surplus, have been shipped to Maine where we will stay for the summer, preparing for the wedding.

Heading back east, we are filled with conflicting emotions. New York both attracts and repels us, spinning our heads with confusion; on top of this, the wedding is approaching at an alarming pace. We've designated the wedding weekend as the end of our year of the goat, and the closer it gets, the more we know that we need a next plan. In truth, the feeling is a little like college graduation, a time fraught with possibilities that are both energizing and overwhelming. Approaching the city, we are completely in flux.

"Can we really do this?" we ask each other periodically during the three days it takes to drive from Wichita. The question becomes more urgent as signs to New York appear and we pass turnpike tolls, LeFrak City, the Triborough Bridge. Our stomachs clench with the traffic, yellow taxis whizzing within inches of our mirrors as we creep down the East Side Highway. Godfrey, whose head is habitually lolling out of the car, is wrestled back inside; with our bags and boxes packed to the ceiling, I lean out the passenger window to act as a rearview mirror.

We've only been gone from New York for a year, but it feels like an eternity. Now we see the city with new eyes, ones that have become accustomed to a slower, greener, more tranquil view. Staying in midtown with Karl's aunt, we take Godfrey for a walk and are shocked by how difficult it is to find him a patch of grass on which to pee. Riding the subway downtown to meet some friends for drinks, the shriek of metal startles us so much that we cover our ears. Once settled comfortably in the velvet banquette of a dark lounge, we're horrified by the price of cocktails and tally in our heads how much goat feed could be bought with our bar tab. Throughout the evening, we bore our friends with talk of heritage animal breeds, raw-milk legislation, and agricultural tariffs.

Many things in the city now surprise us. Quality cheese can be bought at every turn—Murray's, both in the Village and at its outpost in Grand Central Station; Artisanal in Midtown; even a place near my old apartment in Williamsburg, where three years earlier I couldn't find an English-language newspaper. Farmers' markets abound and sell meats and cheeses next to mounds of fresh produce; in a year, the fledgling strip of stalls that had just begun near our apartment in Fort Greene has become a neighborhood fixture.

Although we don't make it to a restaurant we've heard is serving goat in the Meatpacking District, we do look for goat meat in every bodega we pass and find it in markets from the Lower East Side to the Upper West. On a clear blue morning, we take a train to the Bronx to visit Musa Slaughterhouse. Run by Gambian Muslims, the store is a microcosm of the neighborhood, a *halal carnicería* that caters to both the Islamic and the Latino members of the community. Stretching half a block in a series of cinder-block storefronts, Musa's sells caged chickens and rabbits out of one shop, ready-butchered meats out of another. Through a third doorway, we find live goats, sheep, and one lonely cow squeezed into storefront pens. The animals are in terrible shape—visibly malnourished, runny eyed—but there is clearly a market for their meat.

Signs in the windows read "You pick them . . . we kill them" and "All halal killed." In red block lettering, one shouts WE ROAST; two others remind patrons to order their lamb, goats, and cows for the holidays. Several are in Spanish: "Tenemos carnes de res, chivo y lamb," "Frescas y a los mejores precios."

The place advertises that it is USDA inspected, but based on the condition of the animals and the dubious meat counter we are skeptical. Inside no one will speak to us except a tall, deeply dark man in a crocheted skullcap and battered wellies who is watering the animals. I offer him the colloquial greeting I remember from the Gambian bakers at Magnolia.

"Nanga def?" I ask. How's it going?

"Yamaray," he answers, giving us a shy, confused smile before retreating behind swinging doors. Moments later several more men emerge and ask in halting English what we want. There is no satisfactory answer we can give, so we beat a hasty retreat, taking a few photos from across the street before scurrying back to the subway.

Has this much goat been here all along? As in the months before we left on our journey, we seem to find goats around every New York corner. But now, instead of piquing our curiosity, these goat glimpses make us long for them. Everything we want we can get in the city, except the quiet and comfort of the animals. Nearly a year after our departure, we realize that we have gone for good.

Over the following days, we are blessed with crystalline skies and temperate heat as we revisit our favorite corners of the city and reconnect with friends. We walk Godfrey in Central Park, waiting with him beneath the zoo's clock for the hour to strike and send the dancing goat spinning. In Chelsea, my friend Billy has opened a bakery, and we spend a glorious hour tasting his cakes and pies. Farther downtown, in Chinatown for dim sum, we notice a few faded decals celebrating the Year of the Monkey. This visual reminder is startling. It is with bittersweet feelings that we see how much time has passed.

Late one morning during our stay, in a little café on Avenue B, a dozen of my friends gather for a bridal shower. Some have flown in from as far away as California, while others have walked over from their apartments nearby. We drink mimosas and open elaborately wrapped presents, and for this one morning, without Karl, caught up in a bubble of future and past, dreams and nostalgia, I forget the goats.

My friends and I sit around tables we've pushed together, a kaleidoscope of lives as bright and jumbled as the city we're in or the country I've just explored. We are single and attached, male and female, gay and straight. We are happy with our lives, seeking different paths, just trying to figure it all out. In the city I've been trimmed, waxed, manicured, and unlike San Francisco where I felt secretly like a fake, here I know how to belong. We're laughing, urbane, reminiscing about our shared pasts, and it feels good. I know that the future I've chosen will be far different from this scene, but there's comfort in its familiarity. I don't miss this life enough to move back to New York, to abandon the goat dreams for a MetroCard and a pair of Manolo Blahniks. But a part of me will always love the city.

The morning before we leave for Maine, Karl and I meet my friend Shawn for breakfast on the Upper East Side. We have one final mission in the city: to find a goat-print tie in which Karl can be married.

We have scoured every store we can think of: Thomas Pink's (full of foxes), Hermès (saddles and stirrups), Brooks Brothers (rep ties and many sheep). Fashion is the one corner of New York that goats seem not to have penetrated.

At Shawn's suggestion we try Bloomingdale's after breakfast, which at first seems like another bust. The three of us wander menswear, disturbing great wheels of ties to finger any one that looks vaguely animal. Finally, we approach a tired-looking salesman.

"I know this is an odd request," I begin, my nervous voice rising to a squeak, "But we were wondering if you had any ties printed with goats?"

His answer is completely unexpected. Salvatore Ferragamo had made a goat-print tie two seasons ago—"I remember because my niece raises goats in Vermont." There were several colors, he says, poking around for them in the ties under his glass counter. It looks like they're out of them at Bloomingdales, he apologizes, but we should try the Ferragamo store on Madison.

By this point it has begun to rain. Shawn has an appointment, but Karl and I press on, dashing between awnings until we come to Ferragamo's glass façade. On the first floor, our request is greeted by a cool sneer from a severe-looking but impeccably dressed saleswoman. Upstairs, however, a young man disappears into the back, and though he returns empty-handed, he has several suggestions. The outlet shop at Woodbury Common, he thinks, will be our best bet.

We are deflated, needing to get on the road but debating whether to drive to the suburbs in pursuit of this elusive tie. The wild goat chase is quickly becoming an obsession; we're just a few blocks from Saks, so we decide to give it one last try. Riding the escalators, we vow that this will be our final stop.

Upstairs, there is a huge sale in menswear and the overworked staff has become snappish. We search racks and tables of ties but find nothing and finally look for someone to ask. A harried saleswoman with a thick, Eastern European accent assures us that she has not seen any goats. We decide that this is it—we give up. On our way out, though, we stop to paw through one last bin of sale items. We push aside a tangle of bow ties, cloth suspenders, and ascots. The bin is a jumble of prints. And there, at the very bottom, is a single navy blue Ferragamo tie printed with tiny beige goats. Not only have we found it, but it's on sale.

In the fall of 2005, goats will take over Saks for a promotion they call Wild About Cashmere. There will be goats in every display window, an outrageously expensive commemorative stuffed goat, and a children's book printed for the occasion about a family of silvery cashmere goats from Mongolia. Karl will go down to New York to photograph Wendy Pieh and a trailer of her animals, which Saks has rented for an ad campaign in which models wearing tight white jeans and bright pink T-shirts that read "Wild About Cashmere" walk the goats throughout midtown Manhattan. This is the glorious future, however; in the present, we're lucky to find one goat tie.

Outside, the weather has cleared and the pavement is drying. We are walking on air. Rounding the corner onto Madison, the helpful clerk from the Ferragamo store is strolling along with a sandwich, and we run up to show him the tie. In a gesture that seems almost displaced in the city, he beams and offers us his hand in congratulations.

Chapter 21

While we were on the road, visiting so many agricultural communities, Karl and I often asked each other, "Could we live here? Could we imagine ourselves as part of this community? Could we raise a family, milk some goats, and keep ourselves intellectually sustained in this corner of the world?" We had started our journey, after all, as city folk, and as much as we wanted to live an agricultural life, we also knew that we needed other kinds of stimulation: spontaneous conversation, a good coffee shop, proximity to museums, interesting restaurants, and at least one independent bookstore. In short, we wanted a cultural, as well as an agricultural, existence.

Overwhelmingly when we asked ourselves these questions we could answer them in the affirmative. In northern California, southern Indiana, even central Texas we found land that was beautiful, towns that were idiosyncratically charming, and people who were both engaging and welcoming. Strangers had opened their homes to us; we'd arrived dusty and disoriented, sometimes at the wrong farmhouse, sometimes late at night, and we'd been fed with cold chicken, offered a bed, given a direction. We'd found political tolerance, religious curiosity, and above all, a true human concern for us, however briefly we were a part of people's lives. From the tow truck driver who saw our license plate and flagged us down outside Plains, Georgia, to give us a calendar from his body shop and tell us how much he loved his one visit to Maine in the mid-seventies; to Yahoo's Goats 101 list serve moderator Vern Charles in Delta, Colorado, who invited us and our unruly dog into her house of prized Scottish Fold cats; to Dolores Vernor who gave us hand-knitted mohair stocking caps to ward off a cold snap when we stopped at her south Texas shop—people took care of us both physically and emotionally, even when we didn't know we needed it. And they did it without any expectation that we would return the favor. They cared for us simply because that's what people do. In our exploration of its back roads and rural outposts, this great country and its constellation of communities shone with an embarrassment of riches.

As educated, politically liberal New Yorkers, we had considered ourselves before our travels to be open-minded and free of prejudice. In truth, however, I'm not sure that we were. We had fallen into a trap, I realize now, of classing America as red and blue, city and country, faithful and un. We had adopted these kinds of simplistic shorthands because they were easy and because from our perch in the city, the deep textures woven through the rest of the country were somehow glossed over and smoothed into stereotype.

Traveling through America, covering more than forty thousand miles in forty-three states, we found that generalizations just don't apply. Rural ranchers turn out to have Ivy League educations, slaughterhouse managers are married to animal rights activists—the country and its inhabitants are complex and compellingly, unfailingly interesting.

And so we realized that to fulfill our criteria it didn't matter where we settled. In some places it might be easier to find a good espresso or eavesdrop on a casual literary reference than in others, but throughout the country, in the most unlikely spots, we found a wealth of possibility.

Ultimately, we choose to live in Maine to be close to Karl's family and to take advantage of the excellent guidance and resources provided by the Maine Organic Farmers and Gardeners Association, the Maine Cheese Guild, and the state extension office. All are accessible and welcoming and we feel, in Maine, that there is a tremendous network of people who can help us succeed in our goat enterprise. We don't plan to begin looking for property until after the wedding, but we know that this is where we want to stay.

The wedding, in all of its lavishly goat-themed glory, is held on August 8, 2004, at Wolfe's Neck Farm, a six-hundred-acre beef cattle farm on the shore of Casco Bay. In a patch of pasture on a low cliff, white chairs fan in a half moon facing the wedding canopy, its birch poles sprouting from pots of live flowers. To the left, a small wire pen holds two pygmy goats; a basket of carrots with feathery green tops rests on its fence post.

The day is hot with cloudless turquoise skies, and as guests begin to arrive, they pick up bottles of iced spring water from a galvanized metal tub. A basket holds daisies made from yellow tulle for the women to tuck in their hair. Together, the guests look like a giant field of flowers.

We walk down the aisle to the soft bleating of goats and a processional tune from a local klezmer band, Karl in his goat tie and I in simple white. The skies stay blue through the ceremony, but near the end the wind picks up, blowing my veil crazily in its gusts. The rabbi has to raise her voice almost to a shout, and our parents start to fidget and exchange nervous glances. Purple clouds sweep in just as Karl steps on the glass and the guests shout "Mazel tov!"

Our marriage begins with a brief downpour—rain pummels the tent, guests shriek as they race under its flaps, the goats bleat loudly with irritation at the wet. Inside the reception has begun; the band is playing and guests sit at tables set with crisp, butter-yellow linens. Our caterer, Leslie, whom we've chosen from afar, is a Slow Food member who has created a menu of regional ingredients: artisanal goat cheeses, seasonal heirloom vegetables, smoked local fish. For wine, she serves South African Goats do Roam. I've baked the cake, a traditional, whiskey-doused British fruitcake wrapped in marzipan, slathered in royal icing, and topped with two plastic goats. Between one's horns, I've glued a little white veil.

When the skies have cleared, still wearing our wedding clothes, Karl and I open the pen and take the goats for a walk, strolling with them on leashes and letting them munch the flowers at the base of the chuppah. The grass is a vivid green from the rain, the tide is high, the water a sparkling blue. Children are dancing in the field to "Had Gadya," a Yiddish song about a little goat, and some guests have begun to play croquet.

At the edge of the cliff, Karl and I look out at the water and know that we've started a new goat journey. Before us, there's a rainbow over the ocean.

Epilogue

After the wedding, Karl and I spent our first few days of married life at the Squire Tarbox Inn, a small bed-and-breakfast on the coast of Maine that serves food grown in its own garden and keeps a small herd of goats in a barn out back. Under the previous owners, the inn had made goat cheese, but by the time we stayed there the animals were simply for character and the equipment was for sale. While this seemed an auspicious sign—we could come back from our abridged honeymoon with a pasteurizer and milk tank!—we had decided to be methodical in our pursuit. If we had learned anything from our travels, it was that there were great risks attached to jumping into a farming enterprise. The most successful farms we'd visited were ones that adhered to the basic and sound principles of small business. They had a business plan, bit off projects and debt in digestible amounts, and above all, they did research.

And so, instead of immediately buying equipment, we drew up our five-year goals, attended a business-plan-writing seminar at the state agricultural trade fair, and found paying jobs. We rented a small apartment in the center of Portland and retired the Goat Mobile as much as possible, walking almost everywhere. Godfrey became a fixture in our neighborhood, making dog and people friends along every block. We became deeply involved with the Maine Organic Farmers and Gardeners Association, began volunteering at Wolfe's Neck Farm, and were founding members of the Portland Slow Food Convivium. On weekends, we started canvassing the state for property.

After our visit to Quillisascut in Washington state, we had become very interested in environmentally friendly, "green" methods of building, and in particular, straw bale construction like the retreat house Rick Misterly had built. With this in mind, we started our search by looking for property on which to build. An architect on the board at Wolfe's Neck recommended a colleague who was a straw bale enthusiast, and we met with him several times to create plans for a small, loftlike house, something we could shepherd through construction on our own. With his direction, we priced composting toilets, looked into drainage systems, and debated whether a Murphy bed would be the most efficient use of bedroom space. We got ahead of ourselves, of course, but researching this kind of minutia was thrilling; every day brought new ideas and knowledge about things we'd never before considered. We could carve a feeding trough into an outer wall, use filled bookshelves as an extra layer of insulation, build cupboards into the staircase. Our experiences in small New York apartments served us well as we considered how to maximize every inch of space. What we were trying to build, really, was a studio apartment that we were hoping to set in the middle of a pasture.

For building materials, we looked locally, speaking about the carpentry with a young cabinetmaker who worked with salvaged materials, and trolling antique stores and shops that specialized in vintage hardware for drawer pulls and doorknobs. Through a baker who was one of Slow Food Portland's core members, we found several small farmers near the Canadian border in Aroostook County who were growing wheat and had bales of straw to sell.

"Before it was known for potatoes," the baker told us with a sigh, "northern Maine was actually considered the breadbasket of New England. Most of the wheat on the East Coast came from Maine until the late 1800s, and then trains started bringing it from the Midwest. After that, our farmers switched to potatoes, which of course now are also being farmed in the West." Our friend bought much of the wheat for his bakeries from local sources, he said, from farmers who were once more cultivating varieties favored during the Civil War.

These sorts of details about Maine's agricultural history made us even more excited about becoming a part of it. We followed every lead for land, scouring the online and newspaper real estate listings during the week, then dusting off the Goat Mobile to take weekend drives across the state, checking out the properties in person.

After a few months of searching, we found what seemed to be a promising parcel: thirty-three acres of rolling pasture on the banks of the Androscoggin River. It was a wide swath of field, edged along the river with a strip of woods. There were bluffs our goats could climb, and a fertile plain with soil enriched by the river's centennial flooding. A path led to the water across a little bridge, spanning a small marsh that looked like it had been lifted from an illustration of *The Wind in the Willows*. On our first visit, we saw a beaver swimming through the cattails. The owner raised oxen and Percheron horses, and we discovered that we had mutual friends, all of whom vouched for his character. It seemed perfect; we were in love.

We thought we'd found our farm, and for six months we called off our search to pursue the preliminary surveys, soil testing, and farm loan applications. It seemed so close that we abandoned all caution—we truly felt like we were there already, farming, struggling through the commonplace crises of the agricultural existence while building our goat herd and our life together. We visited the land on weekends, dropped in occasionally on the owner, even went to a baseball game with him.

And then negotiations fell through. The owner simply wanted more money than we were prepared to pay, almost double the assessed price of comparable land. Even if we had tried, no bank would have given us a mortgage, and had we bought the land, there would have been no money left to build on it. As much as we wanted the sale to work, we knew that its terms were such that we would be making a monumental mistake.

To say that we were disappointed would be a gross understatement. We had wanted desperately—maybe too desperately—for this patch of Maine to become our farm. We were tired of waiting, of living vicariously through our farming friends, of sitting over the street in our apartment's bay window, studying books on goat care and poultry management. We were ready, past ready, to muddy our hands and sink our roots into the earth.

In the sale's dissolving wake, I cried a lot; Karl balanced and rebalanced our checkbook. We had invested our time, our money, and, though it sounds melodramatic, we'd invested our dreams in this property. We felt like we were giving up—or even more like we were failing—but deep in our hearts, we knew that we were doing the right thing to walk away. It was still very hard.

At the end of the summer, when we had been in Portland for a little more than a year, we felt resigned. In some respects, we had found what we sought and were in fact part of a greater agricultural community. But we were still living in the middle of a city, parking on the street, shoveling the stoop, owning no animals but Godfrey (and Panzer's horn, which to this day we keep in a box in Karl's dresser). We tried to stay upbeat, but at the beginning of September we were both incredibly depressed.

Then one day, while we were in the middle of this listlessness and despondence, we received a notice from Slow Food International announcing that the Cheese! festival, held biennially in Bra, Italy, would this year be devoted to goats. We were stunned. It was too wonderful to believe! We needed goats to shake us out of this funk, and there they were.

In the middle of September, we flew to Milan, borrowed a car from some Italian friends, and drove to the Piedmont region. There, we stayed at Casa Scaparone, an *agriturismo* (a farmhouse bed-and-breakfast) on a centuries-old estate that was now a working goat farm and vineyard. From our bedroom window, we looked out on fertile hills of hazelnut trees and grapevines; in the morning we woke to a dawn chorus of crowing roosters and faint bleating as the farm's goatherd led the animals down a one-lane road to their pasture. Fruit trees lined the courtyard, and we plucked fresh figs and hard, fuzzy peaches as we walked up the stairs to our room. We were there for the first day of the grape harvest, and we helped pick the fruit, straining our quads and staining our hands a sticky purple.

During the day, we attended Cheese! Though the weather was a drizzling gray and the town was open only to foot traffic, thousands of Italians descended on Bra with their umbrellas, galoshes, and appetites. We joined them, eating goat cheeses from around the world: a pungent Lebanese cheese aged in goatskin, a mild Armenian feta infused with tarragon and aged in terra-cotta pots, a true Norwegian Gjetost, its grainy brown paste pressed into an intricately patterned cube. At tasting seminars, we wore headphones and listened to simultaneous English translations as cheese experts and producers instructed us in their native languages, smacking their tongues into the microphone and guiding our palates through the intricacies of each progressive flavor. At the back of the room, a row of translators sat behind a long table, speaking into their microphones in a cacophonous murmur—it was like some kind of caseous United Nations summit.

The streets of Bra were lined with tents of vendors and representatives of cheese and wine varieties from throughout the world. Slow Food U.S.A. had a booth giving out samples of raw-milk cheeses from the American South, including some made by Judy Schad who was at the festival with Sofia Solomon. Since the booth was short-handed, we helped staff it, trying our pidgin Italian—"Latte crude, Americano, from Texas"—on everyone who stopped by. American cheese was clearly thought of as a curiosity; the booth was sandwiched next to one giving out Tibetan yak's milk cheese that was staffed by monks in saffron robes who presented Carlo Petrini, Slow Food's founder, with a white silk scarf. Everyone who tried our cheese seemed pleasantly shocked, making that pan-European, raised-eyebrow-and-downturned-mouth look of surprise.

"Non male?" we asked encouragingly. Not bad?

A little more than a year after our marriage this trip was our true honeymoon, and it was invigorating. We returned to Maine with syrupy balsamic vinegar, hunks of cheese, and a drying rack for pasta. We also came back revitalized, with a new life—both figuratively and literally, as it turned out.

Immediately upon our return, we began to look once more in earnest for property, expanding our search to include existing houses with smaller acreage. Amazingly, within weeks we'd found a white 1901 clapboard farmhouse with a huge attached red barn on ten acres of land. It was built along the classic New England plan: big house, little house, back house, barn, rambling in a line down the rural route. In the back was a small apple orchard with ten trees; a large, long-neglected paddock and garden; and seven acres of woods. The house had four bedrooms, a library, and a deep stone cellar. In front was a white picket fence, and on each side crumbling stone walls edged the property. It was not energy efficient or compact, but it was glorious. Only half an hour from Portland, it seemed a world away.

We bought the property and moved on a snowy day in December. I was then three months pregnant with our daughter, Charlotte.

The winter passed cozily with fires in the woodstoves and long walks in the woods; reveling in the sweeps of snow, we explored our land and planned for spring. In January we found moles living in our kitchen and adopted Snuppy the cat—an excellent, stealthy stalker—from a local shelter. In February an agent from the extension office came out to give us advice about rehabilitating the property for agricultural production.

We bought our first four Alpine goats from one of our favorite Maine cheese makers, Cheese Guild president Caitlin Hunter of Appleton Creamery. During kidding season, under the flat skies of cold early March, we drove up to her farm to attend the births and picked out two doelings and two tiny bucks. I paid new attention to the laboring does: their grunts and moans, their clear wish for privacy as they turned their faces to the wall and pushed out the babies, the buckets of warm molasses water they guzzled in their postpartum dehydration. After cleaning up the kids—toweling them off, blow-drying their coats—Caitlin wrapped them in soft rags and let us bottle-feed them. Sitting in her barn, trying to coax the rubber nipple of a bottle into our little brown goat's mouth, I felt my own baby kicking and swimming in my belly. Everything felt cosmically right.

Our goats came home at the end of March, all four squeezed into a hay-strewn dog crate in the back of our car. After three years of anticipation, this, more than leaving the city, more than finding the farm, was the fulfillment of our dream. It was strange and exciting, after so much time spent planning for this moment, to finally open the barn doors and wrangle them inside. They capered around and explored, sniffing the bales of hay we'd stacked near their pen, and as Karl and I stood there watching them, it sunk in: we finally had our goats. We were amazed, delighted, and more than a little nervous.

We named the kids for historical figures from Maine: the boys are Percival Baxter and Joshua Lawrence Chamberlain, after two of the state's governors. The girls are Flyrod and Chansonetta, named respectively after Cornelia "Fly Rod" Crosby, the first female certified Maine Guide, and Chansonetta Stanley Emmons, a pioneering turn-of-the-century woman photographer. We will eventually milk the does, and when the boys are a little older, Karl plans to train them to pack using John Mionczynski's instructions. When they were a few months old, we took the bucklings to our vet in downtown Portland and had them wethered. There were some stares as we led them on leashes across the parking lot and street, but several pedestrians also came up to us and asked to pet them. One woman told us that we'd turned her day around.

The goats live in a pen in our barn where Karl built them a wooden manger for eating and a cinder-block pyramid for play. Until their hooves and horns became too hardened, Karl would lean over and let the goats hop from the top of their blocks onto his rounded back, where they would balance and nibble at his hair. Godfrey, who considers himself an honorary goat, would often try to join in, though he weighed considerably more.

For the first few months, we fed the goats milk from a nearby dairy, and each feeding left our sleeves damp and our kitchen a mess of rubber nipples and bottle brushes. Now they've switched to grain and hay, and when the weather is nice, we lead them outside to browse in a mobile pen that we shift around the property. During my seventh month of pregnancy, Percival made several great escapes from the electric fence, and I, heavily pregnant, waddled and wove after him, waving my hands and calling his name until I could lure him back in with a handful of weeds. Another afternoon, I didn't latch their pen securely and turned around to find that Joshua and Flyrod had followed me into the house. The goats are happy and mischievous, affectionate to us, and curious about their surroundings. They are a perpetual adventure.

In April, we ordered twelve heritage breed laying hens from the Ames Farm Center—"A farm store and a whole lot more"—our favorite local store. The chickens arrived at the end of the month, and when John Ames, the proprietor, called to tell us they were in, I was so excited that I almost hopped up and down, pregnant belly and all. We designated one corner of the barn for the birds, putting in nesting boxes, painting a mural of inspirational chickens (laying golden eggs, flying up into the trees), and enclosing the coop with chicken wire. We expected them to be pullets—the poultry equivalent of teenagers—but when I picked them up, they were just a day out of the shell. At the store, I tried to pretend that I wasn't caught off guard, but revealed once more what a novice I was when I had to buy all the equipment for chicks: heat lamp, feeders, a watering contraption, and (most tellingly) a book about raising chickens. There's still a lot we have to learn.

I put the chicks in a box in the back seat and called Karl on my cell phone. In the parking lot of the farm store, I put the phone up to the box. The chicks were huddled in one corner, peeping loudly.

"What's that squeaking noise?" he asked.

"Those are our laying hens."

We clipped a heat lamp to the arm of the rocking chair in the baby nursery, banished Snuppy—who saw the little birds as a buffet—from the upstairs, and brought the chicks inside. They lived for a month in the galvanized metal tub that had held bottled water at our wedding, then moved on to a refrigerator box, and finally into their coop. We cut a chicken door into the side of the barn, and during the day they come outside to scratch around their yard and roost on the stones of our house's foundation. As it turns out, only eleven will lay eggs; one black Australorp matured into a tyrannical rooster we named Larry. He patrols the yard, crowing, all day.

In the late spring, our apple trees budded, and we made pies with the rhubarb that sprang unannounced from a corner of the lawn. We tapped our maple trees and boiled ten gallons of sap down to one jar of syrup. The overgrown garden we tilled and planted with potatoes, tomatoes, greens, and herbs. By then—just weeks before I delivered—I could no longer bend over, so I dug holes with a long-handled shovel and Karl loosened the earth and set our seedlings into the ground. In June we welcomed Charlotte.

Our daughter will grow up on a farm, taking for granted the life that it took us an expedition across America to discover. She will begin her mornings with chores—there will be feed to scatter, goats to milk, kitchen scraps to compost. She will drift to a sound sleep in the quiet of the country. The rhythm of her life will follow the seasons, tiring her with its physical intensity in the summer, gratifying her with its bounty in the fall, slowing to its winter pace as the work turns more cerebral, and then blossoming with possibility each spring. She will blossom with possibility on this farm.

And Karl and I? We've found a way of life that sustains us on all levels, filling our minds and our hearts and our bellies. It's a life that makes us feel whole. We credit the goats: they have brought us this far, and we can only trust that they'll be with us as we continue the journey. Like the vegetables we grow and the cheeses we plan to produce, on this farm we will ripen.

Acknowledgments

Those book chronicles a journey, covering physical, intellectual, and emotional terrain, that I could never have taken alone. It is the work of many, though any errors are entirely my own. Countless hands helped to shape this narrative, and I hope that my deep gratitude is evident from these pages. I'm indebted to everyone who supported and encouraged us, but there are a number of people whose contributions were so considerable that without them this great goat adventure would not have been possible.

Above all, I wish to thank Karl, my husband and partner, for his boundless curiosity, obsessive attention to detail, phenomenal memory, and infinite patience. This has not simply been my journey, it has been ours, and just as he now carefully tends our animals and gardens, Karl has sustained me along the way.

For their unflagging support at every stage, I'm grateful to our families, especially our parents, Jeanine Hathaway, Steve Hathaway, and Bruce and Nancy Schatz. Without their overwhelming generosity, we could never have realized our goat dreams.

Throughout our travels, we were sponsored by several businesses and organizations whose monetary donations kept our project alive: Billy's Bakery, Billy Goat Gruff (Tarter Gates), Wind River Pack Goats, and the American Meat Goat Association. Organizations that have lent us their support and resources include the American Dairy Goat Association, the International Goat Days Family Festival, the Maine Organic Farmers and Gardeners Association, Slow Food USA, and Wolfe's Neck Farm. I'd also like to thank everyone who bought *Year of the Goat* T-shirts and puppets through our Web site.

The goat project could never have become a book without the enthusiasm and encouragement of my agent, Jill Grinberg, and her associate Kirsten Wolf. I'm honored that they believed in this story and will be forever grateful for their advice and advocacy. My editor, Christine Duffy, has been a joy to work with, and her keen eye has brought out the best in our story. I'm thankful, too, for the support of the entire team at The Lyons Press.

Thank you to Bridget Brier and Cynthia Mines for their insightful comments on the manuscript.

For keeping me sane and healthy through the simultaneous gestation of my book and my daughter, I'm grateful to The Back Cove Midwives, especially Leah Coplon and Stacy Brenner. Without them, I'm not sure I could have delivered either.

For setting us on this path, however inadvertently, I'd like to thank Dr. Robert Fraum.

The bulk of my gratitude goes to the many people who opened their lives and homes to us, without whom *The Year of the Goat* would not have been possible. The book is marked with their stories, even if they don't appear in its pages. Thanks to: John Abel and the Tennessee Trash Cookers, the folks at Ames Farm Center, Ada and Jim Austin, Tim and Colleen Avazian, Dave Bernier, Jennifer Bice and everyone at Redwood Hill Farm, the Boehle family, the Bolton family, Richard

Brzozowski, Rabbi Susan Bulba Carvutto, Linda Campbell and Khimaira Web Hosting, Phil and Robert Cassette, LaVerne and Ken Charles, the Circle H Auction, Ruble Conatser, Elaine Considine, Steve Considine, Benny Cox and Producers Livestock, Doug Curle, Dave and Peg Daubert, Levent Demergil and Yuksol Pece, Karyl Dronen, Ken Emrick, Evin Evans and Pat Bell, Nicole Feld and everyone at Ringling Bros. and Barnum & Bailey Circus, Dr. John Flood, Chef John Folse, the Goat Getters 4-H Club of Marion, Kentucky, Debi and Bill Greenberg, Charlie Hancock, Bill Hanks and Al Livingston, Dr. Steven Hart and Dr. Terry Gipson of the E. (Kika) de la Garza Institute for Goat Research at Langston University, Suzy Hassler, Jim Hershberger, Chef Adrian Hoffman, Charles Hopkins, Paul and Marilyn Hopkins, Talib Islam, Lars Johnson and the staff and patrons of Al Johnson's Swedish Restaurant, the Junction Auction, Elizabeth Kennelly, Earl and Marge Kitchen, Larry Krech, Pam Kroll, Russell Libby, Christine and Vince Maefsky, Andrea and Tony Malmberg, Lani Malmberg, Ramón Martínez and the Chicago Cubs organization, Geoff Masterson, Seco Mayfield, Max McCalman, Cindi McDonald, John Mionczynski, Rick and Lora Lea Misterly, Andy Oliver, Ginger Olsen and Diana Livingston, Dean Olsher and Amanda Aronczyk, Leslie Oster and everyone at Aurora Provisions, Joy Peckham, Wendy Pieh and Peter Goth, Pogo, Dr. David Pugh and Dr. Leslie Lawhorn and the Auburn University College of Veterinary Medicine, Callene Rapp and the Sedgwick County Zoo, Judy and Larry Schad, Enid Schatz and David Mitchell, Jim Schott, Marvin Shurley, Sam Sianis, Karen Smith, Sofia Solomon, Ken and Janice Spaulding, Becky and Roger Sweet, Kenneth Thompson, Bret Thorn, Tilton's Auction, Allysa Torey, Joan and Jim Vandergriff, Anton Ward, Carol and Frank Webber, Charlie Wilson, Miss Jeanne and Larry Wilson, Leigh Wilson and Jana Jacobs, and Leslie Wootten and Jerry Baldwin. Special thanks to Caitlin Owen Hunter for all of her guidance and our goats.

Between our travels and the writing of this book, the goat world lost three of its dearest members. We mourn the passing of Nick Shurley, Sara Bolton, and Harvey Considine, and hope that a little of their spirits live on in these pages.